14th Workshop on Natural Language Processing for Computer Assisted Language Learning (NLP4CALL 2025)

Tallinn, Estonia
5 March 2025

Editors:

Ricardo Muñoz Sánchez
David Alfter
Elena Volodina
Jelena Kallas

ISBN: 979-8-3313-1887-1

Printed from e-media with permission by:

Curran Associates, Inc.
57 Morehouse Lane
Red Hook, NY 12571

Some format issues inherent in the e-media version may also appear in this print version.

Association for Computational Linguistics
209 N. Eighth Street
Stroudsburg, Pennsylvania 18360

Phone: 1-570-476-8006
Fax: 1-570-476-0860

acl@aclweb.org

Additional copies of this publication are available from:

Curran Associates, Inc.
57 Morehouse Lane
Red Hook, NY 12571 USA
Phone: 845-758-0400
Fax: 845-758-2633
Email: curran@proceedings.com
Web: www.proceedings.com

Proceedings of the 14th Workshop on Natural Language Processing for Computer Assisted Language Learning (NLP4CALL 2025)

University of Tartu Library

2025

Proceedings of the

14th Workshop on Natural Language Processing for Computer Assisted Language Learning (NLP4CALL 2025)

edited by
Ricardo Muñoz Sánchez, David Alfter, Elena Volodina and Jelena Kallas

University of Tartu Library

2025

Preface

The workshop series on Natural Language Processing (NLP) for Computer-Assisted Language Learning (NLP4CALL) is a meeting place for researchers working on integrating Natural Language Processing and Speech Technologies in CALL systems and exploring the theoretical and methodological issues arising in this connection. The latter includes, among others, the integration of insights from Second Language Acquisition (SLA) research and the promotion of "Computational SLA" through setting up Second Language research infrastructures.

The intersection of Natural Language Processing (or Language Technology / Computational Linguistics) and Speech Technology with Computer-Assisted Language Learning (CALL) brings "understanding" of language to CALL tools, thus making CALL intelligent. This fact has inspired the name for this area of research — Intelligent CALL, ICALL for short. As the definition suggests, apart from having excellent knowledge of Natural Language Processing and/or Speech Technology, ICALL researchers need good insights into second language acquisition theories and practices, as well as knowledge of second language pedagogy and didactics. Therefore, this workshop invites a wide range of ICALL-relevant research, including studies where NLP-enriched tools are used for testing SLA and pedagogical theories, and those where SLA theories (pedagogical practices or empirical data) and modeled using ICALL tools. The NLP4CALL workshop series is aimed at bringing together competences from these areas for sharing experiences and brainstorming around the future of the field.

Topics of Interest

We invited submissions:

- that describe research directly aimed at ICALL;
- that describe the ongoing development of resources and tools with potential usage in ICALL either directly in interactive applications or indirectly in materials, application, or curriculum development (e.g. learning material generation, assessment of learner texts and responses, individualized learning solutions, provision of feedback);
- that discuss challenges and/or research agendas for ICALL;
- that describe empirical studies on language learner data; and
- that explore the use of LLMs and Generative AI to develop ICALL tools.

In this edition of the workshop a special focus was given to:

- grammatical error correction and
- the use of pedagogically oriented constructicographic resources (constructicons), with an emphasis on their practical application in ICALL.[1]

We encouraged paper presentations and software demonstrations describing the above-mentioned themes primarily, but not exclusively, for the Nordic languages.

A special feature in this year's workshop was the MultiGEC-2025 shared task on grammatical error correction that was held in connection to the workshop. It featured 12 European languages (Czech, English, Estonian, German, Greek, Icelandic, Italian, Latvian, Russian, Slovene, Swedish

[1] By constructicographic resources, we refer to resources that describe various types of constructions associated with specific meanings or functions, ranging from fully schematic and semi-schematic constructions (e.g., those with both fixed and variable elements) to specific lexical expressions.

Ricardo Muñoz Sánchez, David Alfter, Elena Volodina and Jelena Kallas. Preface. *Proceedings of the 14th Workshop on Natural Language Processing for Computer Assisted Language Learning (NLP4CALL 2025).* University of Tartu Library. i–vi.

and Ukrainian) and was organized by the CompSLA working group[2] as well as over 20 external data providers. A paper describing the shared task and system descriptions from two of the participating teams are included in these proceedings.

Invited speakers

This year, we had the pleasure to welcome two invited speakers: Andrew Caines (University of Cambridge) and Peter Uhrig (Friedrich-Alexander-Universität Erlangen-Nürnberg).

Andrew Caines is a Senior Research Associate based in the Computer Laboratory at the University of Cambridge, U.K. He has been a member of the Institute for Automated Language Teaching & Assessment (ALTA) since its inception in 2013. His research interests relate to education technology for language learning, including corpus creation, automated essay scoring, grammatical error detection and correction, adaptive learning, content creation, and the training of smaller, domain-specific language models. The title of his talk was *The Potential and the Pitfalls of Very Large Language Models for Language Learning Applications.*

Peter Uhrig is professor of Digital Linguistics with a focus on Big Data at Friedrich-Alexander-Universität Erlangen-Nürnberg. His research interests include cognitive linguistics, especially Construction Grammar, collo-phenomena (collocation, collostruction), computational and corpus linguistics, and lexicography. He is particularly interested in using large multimodal datasets, data science methods, and machine learning in his work. In addition to his research, Peter Uhrig is committed to creating research infrastructures and open datasets, supporting the broader linguistic community. His work aims to integrate technology with linguistic research, contributing to the evolving field of Digital Linguistics. The title of his talk was *AI-assisted (Pedagogical) Constructicography – Opportunities and Challenges.*

Previous workshops

This workshop follows a series of workshops on NLP4CALL organized by the NEALT Special Interest Group on Intelligent Computer-Assisted Language Learning (SIG-ICALL)[3]. The workshop series has previously been financed by:

- the Center for Language Technology at the University of Gothenburg;
- the SweLL project;[4]
- the Swedish Research Council's conference grant, Språkbanken Text;[5]
- the L2 profiling project;[6]
- itec;[7]
- the CENTAL;[8]
- the Analytics for Language Learning (A4LL) project[9] at LIDILE - Univ Rennes;

[2] https://spraakbanken.gu.se/compsla
[3] https://spraakbanken.gu.se/en/research/themes/icall/sig-icall
[4] https://spraakbanken.gu.se/en/projects/swell
[5] https://spraakbanken.gu.se
[6] https://spraakbanken.gu.se/en/projects/l2profiles
[7] https://itec.kuleuven-kulak.be
[8] https://cental.uclouvain.be
[9] https://sites-recherche.univ-rennes2.fr/lidile/articles/a4all/

- the Mormor Karl project;[10] and
- the project "Expanding the scope of a multi-purpose lexicographic resource to grammar and L2 competence".[11]

Submissions to the fourteen workshop editions have targeted a wide range of languages, ranging from well-resourced languages (Chinese, German, English, French, Portuguese, Russian, Spanish) to lesser-resourced languages (Erzya, Arabic, Estonian, Irish, Komi-Zyrian, Meadow Mari, Saami, Udmurt, Võro). Among these, several Nordic languages have been targeted, namely Danish, Estonian, Finnish, Icelandic, Norwegian, Saami, Swedish and Võro. The wide scope of the workshop is also evident in the affiliations of the participating authors as illustrated in Table 1.

The acceptance rate has varied between 44% and 82%, the average being 63% (see Table 2). Although the acceptance rate is rather high, the reviewing process has always been very rigorous with two to three double-blind reviews per submission. This indicates that submissions to the workshop have usually been of high quality.

Country	**Count**	**Country**	**Count**
Algeria	1	Japan	7
Australia	2	Lithuania	1
Belgium	20	Netherlands	4
Canada	4	Norway	16
China	5	Poland	1
Cyprus	3	Portugal	8
Czech Republic	1	Romania	1
Denmark	5	Russia	10
Egypt	1	Slovakia	1
Estonia	3	Spain	5
Finland	15	Sweden	87
France	35	Switzerland	15
Germany	135	Ukraine	2
Iceland	6	UK	25
Ireland	5	Uruguay	5
Israel	1	US	15
Italy	15	Vietnam	3

Table 1: NLP4CALL speakers' and co-authors' affiliations, 2012–2025

[10] `https://mormor-karl.github.io/`
[11] `https://eki.ee/prg-1978/`

Workshop year	Submitted	Accepted	Acceptance rate
2012	12	8	67%
2013	8	4	50%
2014	13	13	77%
2015	9	6	67%
2016	14	10	72%
2017	13	7	54%
2018	16	11	69%
2019	16	10	63%
2020	7	4	57%
2021	11	6	54%
2022	23	13	56%
2023	18	12	67%
2024	23	19	82%
2025	16	7	44%

Table 2: Submissions and acceptance rates, 2012–2025

Program committee

We would like to thank our Program Committee for providing detailed feedback for the reviewed papers:

- David Alfter, University of Gothenburg, Sweden
- Serge Bibauw, Universidad Central del Ecuador, Ecuador
- Claudia Borg, University of Malta, Malta
- Christopher Bryant, University of Cambridge, UK
- Andrew Caines, University of Cambridge, UK
- Orphée De Clercq, Ghent University, Belgium
- Kordula de Kuthy, Universität Tübingen, Germany
- Piet Desmet, K.U. Leuven, Belgium
- Thomas François, Université catholique de Louvain, Belgium
- Thomas Gaillat, Université Rennes 2, France
- Andrea Horbach, FernUniversität Hagen, Germany
- Jelena Kallas, Institute of the Estonian Language, Estonia
- Joni Kruijsbergen, Ghent University, Belgium
- Murathan Kurfalı, RISE Research Institutes of Sweden, Sweden
- Herbert Lange, University of Gothenburg, Sweden
- Arianna Masciolini, University of Gothenburg, Sweden
- Margot Mieskes, University of Applied Sciences Darmstadt, Germany
- Ricardo Muñoz Sánchez, University of Gothenburg, Sweden
- Lionel Nicolas, EURAC research, Italy
- Ulrike Pado, Hochschule für Technik Stuttgart, Germany
- Magali Paquot, Université catholique de Louvain, Belgium
- Ildikó Pilán, Norwegian Computing Center, Norway
- Gerold Schneider, University of Zurich, Switzerland
- Maria Irena Szawerna, University of Gothenburg, Sweden
- Irina Temnikova, Big Data for Smart Society Institute (GATE)
- Sowmya Vajjala, National Research Council, Canada
- Elena Volodina, University of Gothenburg, Sweden

- Torsten Zesch, FernUniversität Hagen, Germany
- Robert Östling, Stockholm University, Sweden

We intend to continue this workshop series, which so far has been the only ICALL-related recurring event based in the Nordic countries. Our intention is to co-locate the workshop series with the two major LT events in Scandinavia, the Swedish Language Technology Conference (SLTC) and the Nordic Conference on Computational Linguistics (NoDaLiDa), thus making this workshop an annual event. Through this workshop, we intend to profile ICALL research in Nordic countries as weell as beyond, and we aim at providing a dissemination venue for researchers active in this area.

Workshop website

`https://spraakbanken.gu.se/en/research/themes/icall/nlp4call-workshop-series/nlp4call2025`

Workshop organizers

- Ricardo Muñoz Sánchez, Språkbanken Text, University of Gothenburg, Sweden
- David Alfter, Gothenburg Research Infrastructure in Digital Humanities (GRIDH), University of Gothenburg, Sweden
- Elena Volodina, Språkbanken Text, University of Gothenburg, Sweden
- Jelena Kallas, Institute of the Estonian Language, Estonia

Acknowledgments

The 2025 edition of this workshop was supported jointly by:

- The project *Expanding the scope of a multi-purpose lexicographic resource to grammar and L2 competence*,[12] funded by the Estonian Research Council[13] grant (PRG 1978).
- The project *Grandma Karl is 27 years old: Automatic pseudonymization of research data*[14] with the Swedish Research Council[15] grant with funding number 2022-02311.
- The research infrastructure Språkbanken,[16] jointly funded by its 10 partner institutions and the Swedish Research Council (2018–2024; dnr 2017-00626)

[12] `https://eki.ee/prg-1978/`
[13] `https://etag.ee/en/`
[14] `https://mormor-karl.github.io/`
[15] `https://www.vr.se/english.html`
[16] `https://spraakbanken.gu.se/`

Content

The MultiGEC-2025 Shared Task on Multilingual Grammatical Error Correction at NLP4CALL

Arianna Masciolini[1] **Andrew Caines**[2] **Orphée De Clercq**[3] **Joni Kruijsbergen**[3] **Murathan Kurfalı**[5] **Ricardo Muñoz Sánchez**[1] **Elena Volodina**[1] **Robert Östling**[4]

[1]Språkbanken Text, SFS, University of Gothenburg, Sweden
[2]ALTA Institute & Computer Laboratory, University of Cambridge, U.K.
[3]Language and Translation Technology Team, Ghent University, Belgium
[4]Department of Linguistics, Stockholm University, Sweden
[5]RISE Research Institutes of Sweden, Stockholm, Sweden

multigec@svenska.gu.se

Abstract

This paper reports on MultiGEC-2025, the first shared task in text-level Multilingual Grammatical Error Correction. The shared task features twelve European languages (Czech, English, Estonian, German, Greek, Icelandic, Italian, Latvian, Russian, Slovene, Swedish and Ukrainian) and is organized into two tracks, one for systems producing minimally corrected texts, thus preserving as much as possible of the original language use, and one dedicated to systems that prioritize fluency and idiomaticity. We introduce the task setup, data, evaluation metrics and baseline; present results obtained by the submitted systems and discuss key takeaways and ideas for future work.

1 Introduction

Following the successful 2023 shared task on Multilingual Grammatical Error Detection (Volodina et al., 2023), the Computational Second Language Acquisition (CompSLA) working group[1] presents MultiGEC-2025, a shared task in Multilingual Grammatical Error Correction.[2]

In the same vein as the previous task, the main objective of MultiGEC-2025 is to raise interest in NLP for lower-resourced languages. The task features no less than twelve European languages – namely Czech, English, Estonian, German, Greek, Icelandic, Italian, Latvian, Russian, Slovene, Swedish and Ukrainian.

Contrary to traditional GEC resources, the MultiGEC dataset employed for the shared task (Masciolini et al., 2025a,b) consists of full texts. This is intended as an incentive for the development of systems able to take into account contexts larger than individual sentences.

Moreover, we distinguish a "minimal edits" and a "fluency edits" track. Minimal corrections are meant to result in texts that conform to the norms of the target language whilst preserving not only the intended meaning of the original text, but also as much as possible of its original grammar, lexis and writing style (Rudebeck and Sundberg, 2021). Fluency edits, on the other hand, may also include more extensive rephrasings aimed at producing more idiomatic language.

Evaluation is one of the biggest challenges in the organization of a shared task. The presence of the two distinct tracks mentioned above calls for using a mixture of reference-based and reference-free metrics. In addition, all automatic evaluation metrics need to be cross-lingually applicable and to work at the text level. In this paper, we propose three such evaluation metrics that were adapted for the shared task, as well as a one-shot multilingual LLM-based baseline.

An ulterior challenge is encouraging active participation, both within the short time frame of the competitive phase and beyond it, by making the dataset compiled for the shared task easily available in the long term.[3] All in all, we gathered system submissions from four different teams during the competitive phase, three of which worked with all twelve MultiGEC languages. At the time of writing, we also have received about fifty applica-

[1]spraakbanken.gu.se/en/compsla

[2]spraakbanken.gu.se/en/compsla/multigec-2025

[3]The MultiGEC data is available for download at lt3.ugent.be/resources/multigec-dataset.

Arianna Masciolini, Andrew Caines, Orphée De Clercq, Joni Kruijsbergen, Murathan Kurfalı, Ricardo Muñoz Sánchez, Elena Volodina and Robert Östling. The MultiGEC-2025 Shared Task on Multilingual Grammatical Error Correction at NLP4CALL. *Proceedings of the 14th Workshop on Natural Language Processing for Computer Assisted Language Learning (NLP4CALL 2025).* University of Tartu Library. 1–33.

Original

Hello Cristina! I am sorry to hear about you. How are you now? You got relief from your pain and how many weeks are you in the bed? I wish you will well soon.

Minimally corrected reference	**Fluency-edited reference**
Hello Cristina! I am sorry to hear about you. How are you now? You got relief from your pain, and how many weeks are you **in bed**? I **hope** you will **be** well soon.	Hello Cristina! I **was** sorry to hear about **your illness**. How are you now? **Did you get any relief** from your pain, and how many weeks **have** you **been in bed**? I **hope** you will **get better** soon.

Figure 1: Excerpt of a text from the Write & Improve corpus alongside a minimal correction and a fluency-edited version. Note that the latter was produced as an example for this paper and is not part of the subcorpus itself.

tions for data access (over ten of which after the end of the competition), which clearly indicates a broader interest in multilingual data and on the task of GEC.

The remainder of this paper is structured as follows. Section 2 starts with a more detailed description of the task and its two tracks, followed by an overview of the MultiGEC dataset (Section 2.1), an in-depth discussion of the three evaluation metrics selected for the task and their adaptation to our highly multilingual scenario (Section 2.2), as well as a description of our baseline system (Section 2.3). In Section 3, we briefly introduce the submitted systems and present the results they ontained in the competition. We reserve Section 4 for a discussion of the main takeaways from organizing and running this second shared task. Our conclusions, alongside some ideas for future work, are summarized in Section 5.

2 Task Setup

In modern NLP, GEC is a sequence-to-sequence task where the input is a possibly ungrammatical text, typically written by a learner, and the output a normalized or corrected version of the same text. As mentioned in the introduction, the MultiGEC-2025 shared task is organized into two tracks, each corresponding to a particular approach to correction (cf. Figure 1 for an example text corrected in both styles).

For Track 1, the goal is to rewrite texts to make them grammatically correct, i.e. adhering to the norms of the target language without altering the writing style of the original unless strictly necessary, thus following a "minimal edits" principle. Track 2, on the other hand, welcomes systems producing fluency-edited texts, i.e. corrections that are both grammatical and idiomatic.

Both tracks frame GEC as a text-level task. This was done in an attempt to stimulate the development of systems able to take into account contexts larger than traditional sentences, following a recent trend set by the widespread use of LLMs (e.g. Coyne et al. (2023); Loem et al. (2023); Fang et al. (2023); Davis et al. (2024)), which have much larger context windows than the previously dominant translation-based models for GEC (e.g. Brockett et al. (2006); Junczys-Dowmunt and Grundkiewicz (2014); Yuan et al. (2016)).

2.1 Data

We provide training, development and test data for twelve European languages (Czech, English, Estonian, German, Greek, Icelandic, Italian, Latvian, Russian, Slovene, Swedish and Ukrainian) ranging from very high- to low-resourced. The data is organized into seventeen different subcorpora, all derived from pre-existing resources and compiled together into the MultiGEC dataset (Masciolini et al., 2025a,b). Table 1 provides an overview of the datasets in terms of target languages, source corpora, authorship, split sizes, amount of available correction hypothesis sets and correction styles.

As can be inferred from the table, texts come from a variety of sources. For most datasets, the authors of the texts are second language (L2) learners of the target language. This is a direct consequence of the main area of interest of the Computational SLA working group. There are, however, numerous exceptions: some of the

Language code	Subcorpus name	Source corpus	Learners	# essays (train)	# essays (dev)	# essays (test)	Ref. sets	Minimal	Fluency
cs	NatWebInf	Náplava et al. (2022)	L1	3620	1291	1256	2	✓	
	Romani		L1	3247	179	173	2	✓	
	SecLearn		L2	2057	173	177	2	✓	
	NatForm		L1	227	88	76	2	✓	
en	Write & Improve	Nicholls et al. (2024)	L2	4040	506	504	1	✓	
et	EIC	`elle.tlu.ee`	L2	206	26	26	3	✓	✓
	EKIL2	`github.com/tlu-dt-nlp/EstGEC-L2-Corpus`	L2	1202	150	151	2		✓
de	Merlin	Wisniewski et al. (2013), Boyd et al. (2014)	L2	827	103	103	1	✓	
el	GLCII	Tantos et al. (2023)	L2	1031	129	129	1	✓	
is	IceEC	Ingason et al. (2021)	L1	140	18	18	1		✓
	IceL2EC	Ingason et al. (2022)	L2	155	19	19	1		✓
it	Merlin	Wisniewski et al. (2013), Boyd et al. (2014)	L2	651	81	81	1	✓	
lv	LaVA	Darģis et al. (2020), Darģis et al. (2022)	L2	813	101	101	1	✓	
ru	RULEC-GEC	Rozovskaya and Roth (2019)	mixed	2539	1969	1535	3	✓	✓
sl	Solar-Eval	Gantar et al. (2023)	L1	10	50	49	1	✓	
sv	SweLL_gold	Volodina et al. (2019), Volodina et al. (2022)	L2	402	50	50	1	✓	
uk	UA-GEC	Syvokon et al. (2023)	mixed	1706	87	79	4	✓	✓

Table 1: Overview of the MultiGEC-2025 dataset.

Czech, Icelandic and Slovene subcorpora exclusively consist of native speaker (L1) productions – the authors being often, but not always, school children; the Russian corpus comprises essays written by both L2 and heritage speakers and the Ukrainian portion of the dataset is crowdsourced, with no information about the language background of the authors available. Additionally, proficiency levels, text genres, text lengths and subcorpus sizes vary widely across languages. On the one hand, the heterogeneity of the data means that results are not always directly comparable between different languages and subcorpora. This diversity, however, also makes it possible to compare performance between different domains and learner types.

Although most of the source corpora are error-coded, annotation is not consistent across languages. Since contemporary GEC only requires parallel texts – the original and corrected versions, often referred to as a *references* – this problem was solved by omitting all original error codes and converting all subcorpora to a simple Markdown-based format consisting of plain-text files in which alignments are indicated through essay identifiers. Notably, multiple alternative correction hypotheses are available for some of the languages (namely Czech, Estonian, Russian and Ukrainian). Corpora with multiple references are especially valuable because the reliability of reference-based metrics increases when more correction hypotheses are available (see Section 2.2).

The MultiGEC-2025 dataset is now available as a separate resource to enable future work on GEC for all languages included in the task (Masciolini et al., 2025b).[4] Alongside the data, we provide scripts to validate, parse and generate files in this format, as well as all of the evaluation scripts used in the shared task.[5] It must be noted that the current dataset release does not include gold corrections for the test splits. Evaluation of system hypotheses for test data, however, can be carried out on CodaLab[6] using one of the three evaluation metrics employed in the shared task – the GLEU score (see below).

2.2 Evaluation Metrics

As with other text generation tasks, the evaluation of GEC may be approached with reference-based or reference-free methods (Bryant et al., 2023). Reference-based evaluation metrics compare correction hypotheses to a gold standard obtained from human experts. Reference-free met-

[4]Download page: `lt3.ugent.be/resources/multigec-dataset`.

[5]`github.com/spraakbanken/multigec-2025/tree/main/scripts`

[6]`codalab.lisn.upsaclay.fr/competitions/20500`

rics, on the other hand, are important because they enable the evaluation of model output without relying on a single (or, at best, a few) gold-standard correction. This flexibility has become essential with the increasing popularity of LLMs in GEC, as these models are able to generate more varied but still valid corrections that may not align with human references (Östling et al., 2024). Reference-free evaluation methods were thus recently proposed as a way to estimate the quality of system output without relying on gold-standard annotations (cf. Napoles et al. (2016b); Asano et al. (2017); Choshen and Abend (2018); Yoshimura et al. (2020); Islam and Magnani (2021); Maeda et al. (2022)).

For the MultiGEC-2025 shared task, we have opted for three of the most widely used GEC evaluation metrics, each of which offers a different perspective on the quality of the proposed corrections. We use two reference-based metrics – ERRANT (Bryant et al., 2017) and GLEU (Napoles et al., 2015, 2016a) – and one reference-free metric: the Scribendi score (Islam and Magnani, 2021).

For both tracks, all system submissions were scored with these three metrics, but for each track one primary metric was chosen to obtain the final ranking. For Track 1 (minimal edits), we opted for the ERRANT-based $F_{0.5}$ score, a reference-based metric that weighs recall lower than precision, thus penalizing over-correction. For Track 2, which welcomes extensive rephrasings, we adopted the reference-free Scribendi score. We see GLEU as a useful additional metric as it is somewhere in between ERRANT and Scribendi in terms of strictness: it was designed to reward fluency rather than counting edit operations, but still relies on gold-standard corrections.

A major challenge is the need for cross-language applicability, i.e., the requirement for our scoring algorithms to be able to consistently score system output for all languages in the task. Below, we describe the evaluation metrics and steps taken to ensure that each metric can handle the twelve MultiGEC languages.

2.2.1 Reference-based metrics

The ERRANT scorer The ERRor ANnotation Toolkit (ERRANT) enables reference-based evaluation of GEC, adopting an information retrieval approach and outputting precision, recall and $F_{0.5}$ scores to represent the quality of hypothesized corrections compared to references (Bryant et al., 2017). For instance, if a system proposes four insertions of a definite article and three of them are in the correct place, then precision is 0.75; if two gold-standard insertions were missed then recall is $\frac{3}{5} = 0.6$. $F_{0.5}$ is used instead of F_1 so that precision is weighted twice as much as recall in the calculation of the F-measure, based on the reasoning that proposing incorrect corrections to learners in downstream applications is more problematic than failing to correct errors.

ERRANT was designed for English and the original implementation is publicly available.[7] It can be adapted to other languages, but in order to take advantage of its error typing and granular scoring functionality, new classification rules should be written to identify different error types (e.g. subject-verb agreement errors, word order errors, etc). Although such work has been carried out for three of the MultiGEC-2025 languages – Czech (Náplava et al., 2022), German (Boyd, 2018) and Greek (Korre et al., 2021), we had neither time nor resources to carry out this exercise for the rest of the languages and wanted to evaluate the various MultiGEC datasets in a consistent fashion. As a stop-gap measure, we added multilingual support in a rudimentary fashion for the automatic alignment of original and corrected texts, upon which holistic scoring depends. It remains to be seen in future work what impact improved adaptation of ERRANT to other languages would have on evaluation scores.

ERRANT uses spaCy[8] for part-of-speech tagging and lemmatization, which are both necessary for the alignment step. Whenever possible, fast, offline UDPipe 1 models (Straka and Straková, 2017), available through spacy-udpipe[9] were applied. In the case of Icelandic, where no such model is available, the UDPipe 2 API (Straka, 2018) was used instead.

GLEU The Generalized Language Evaluation Understanding score (GLEU) (Napoles et al., 2015, 2016a) is a reference-based metric adapted from the Bilingual Language Evaluation Understanding score (BLEU) used in MT (Papineni et al., 2002). The intuition behind GLEU is that it rewards n-grams in the model outputs that appear in the reference text but not in the original in-

[7] `github.com/chrisjbryant/errant`
[8] `spacy.io`
[9] `github.com/TakeLab/spacy-udpipe`

Original
Hello Cristina! I am sorry to hear about you. How are you now? You got relief from your pain and how many weeks are you in the bed? I wish you will well soon.

Gold reference
Hello Cristina! I am sorry to hear about you. How are you now? You got relief from your pain**,** and how many weeks are you **in bed**? I **hope** you will **be** well soon.

System hypothesis
Hello Cristina! I am sorry to hear about you. How are you now? You got **some** relief from your **pain and** how many weeks are you **in bed**? I **wish** you will **be** well soon.

Scribendi Scoring
Original perplexity (PPL_{orig}) $= 33.0$
Hypothesis perplexity (PPL_{hypo}) $= 25.75$
Token Sort Ratio (TSR) $= 0.96$
Levenshtein Distance Ratio (LDR) $= 0.9625$
$\max(TSR, LDR) = 0.9625 > 0.8$
$PPL_{hypo} = 25.75 < PPL_{orig} = 33.0$
$\therefore Scribendi = 1$

ERRANT Scoring
true positives (TP) = 2
false positives (FP) = 1
false negatives (FN) = 2

Precision (P) = $TP/(TP + FP) = 2/3 = 0.\dot{6}$
Recall (R) = $TP/(TP + FN) = 2/4 = 0.5$
$F_{0.5} = (1+\beta^2) \cdot \frac{P \cdot R}{(\beta^2 \cdot P)+R} = 2.25 \cdot \frac{0.\dot{3}}{2} = 0.1\dot{6}$

Figure 2: Worked example of ERRANT and Scribendi scoring – using the same original (top) and minimally corrected reference text (left) as in Figure 1. On the right is a created minimal correction hypothesis, in which some but not all of the reference edits have been made (note the failure to insert a comma after *pain* and to replace *hope* with *wish*). In addition, a correction is proposed which is not in the reference (insertion of *some*).

put and penalizes n-grams that are present in both the original and corrected texts but not in the reference(s). Although the GLEU score was initially proposed in Napoles et al. (2015), its implementation is presented in Napoles et al. (2016a), which offers a revised formulation that leads to a more reliable score, regardless of the number of available references. In the MultiGEC-2025 shared task, we use a later implementation by Shota Koyama, which corrects the calculation of precision.[10]

2.2.2 Reference-free metrics

Scribendi The Scribendi score (Islam and Magnani, 2021) is a reference-free metric that evaluates the quality of the corrections through a pretrained language model. The core idea is to use perplexity as a proxy for assessing both the fluency and grammaticality of the output of a GEC system. In language modeling, perplexity measures how well a model predicts a sequence of words in a given text, with lower perplexity scores indicating that the text aligns closely with the language model's predictions. Thus, low perplexity suggests that the target text closely matches the typical language usage captured by the model. Scribendi uses this alignment as an indirect measure of linguistic accuracy.

However, the perplexity score alone does not guarantee quality GEC output as perplexity does not indicate whether the intended meaning in the original text is preserved or not. As such, a GEC model that outputs only a short well-formed sentence in the target language would consistently achieve a perplexity score lower than the original text's. In order to overcome this limitation, Scribendi employs a filtering mechanism based on token ratio and Levenshtein distance and discards any corrections that orthographically deviate too significantly from the original text.

Another advantage of Scribendi is that, as long as it relies on a multilingual model, it is easily applicable to new languages, enabling cross-lingually consistent evaluation across languages which was necessary for the shared task at hand. In our preliminary experiments, we evaluated a wide range of multilingual models, with sizes ranging from 1.7 billion to 9 billion parameters, on synthetically corrupted texts across five languages. We ultimately selected Gemma 2 9B[11], which we found to be the most consistent model.

[10] github.com/shotakoyama/gleu/

[11] huggingface.co/google/gemma-2-9b-it

Scribendi assigns a score of 1, 0, or -1 to each text[12], which indicates whether the corrections lower the perplexity of the original sentence, retain or increase it. Additionally, to ensure that the hypothesis does not deviate too much from the original text, Scribendi employs orthographic similarity metrics, the Token Sort Ratio and the Levenshtein Distance Ratio[13]. If either metric falls below a threshold of 0.8, a score of -1 is assigned, indicating that the correction is too dissimilar from the original text. The overall score is calculated by adding these values across all texts. That is, a higher score indicates a greater proportion of successful corrections, with 1 meaning all corrections improve perplexity, 0 meaning none does and a negative score indicates, overall, more corrections increased the perplexity. However, as a reference-free metric, Scribendi is incapable of assessing the accuracy and quality the corrections – only their fluency and overall grammaticality. A system can achieve a perfect score even by making each sentence slightly more fluent without actually fixing all the grammatical errors.

For calculating our three chosen metrics, we convert all texts to a plain text format with one essay per line. In addition, we segment all texts with the language-agnostic `syntok` package[14] to ensure that pre-tokenized and unprocessed datasets are treated in the same way. In Figure 2 we show how evaluation works for the primary metric in each track – ERRANT for minimal correction, and Scribendi for fluency correction – using the English example from Figure 1 and an artificial 'system hypothesis' for the minimal correction track.

2.3 Baseline

The idea behind our baseline is prompting an LLM with one-shot in-context learning. As demonstrated in Davis et al. (2024), prompting LLMs is a simple but effective way to bootstrap GEC systems. However, building a single baseline for the MultiGEC dataset comes with two additional challenges. On the one hand, just as for evaluation metrics, the heterogeneity of the dataset calls for a highly multilingual model. Furthermore, both the need for reproducibility and the licensing conditions for some of the datasets impose the use of an offline, open source model.

Based on these requirements, our model of choice is the eight billion parameter, instruction-tuned version of Llama 3.1[15] (Grattafiori et al., 2024). Although prompting is only officially supported for a subset of the MultiGEC languages (English, German and Italian), this model has likely been exposed to most if not all of them during training on the continuously updated web-scraped Common Crawl dataset[16]. The latter has been shown to comprise over 170 languages, though about one third represents English data (Ortiz Suárez et al., 2019).

We use a prompt based on Davis et al. (2024), albeit with some modifications whose aim is to clearly specify the target language, distinguish between the two aforementioned correction styles, and try to prevent generation of extra text such as faux explanations:

You are a grammatical error correction tool. Your task is to correct the grammaticality and spelling of the input essay written by a learner of `TARGET LANGUAGE`. `TASK DESCRIPTION`. *Return only the corrected text and nothing more.*

Here, `TARGET LANGUAGE` is the language of the essay at hand, while `TASK DESCRIPTION` varies based on the chosen correction style:

Minimal edits	Fluency edits
Make the smallest possible change in order to make the essay grammatically correct. Change as few words as possible. Do not rephrase parts of the essay that are already grammatical. Do not change the meaning of the essay by adding or removing information. If the essay is already grammatically correct, you should output the original essay without changing anything.	*You may rephrase parts of the essay to improve fluency. Do not change the meaning of the essay by adding or removing information. If the essay is already grammatically correct and fluent, you should output the original essay without changing anything.*

To further mitigate format issues in the system output, we also include a single artificial input-output pair in English, thus resulting in a one-shot-baseline.

In addition to this LLM-based system, part of the evaluation also makes use of a "dummy" zero-edit baseline. This is only relevant for establishing a lower bound for GLEU-based scoring (cf. Fig-

[12]The unit of analysis can be adjusted to any level, e.g. sentence, paragraph etc., but is set to full texts in our evaluation.

[13]See Islam and Magnani (2021) for details.

[14]`github.com/fnl/syntok`

[15]`huggingface.co/meta-llama/Llama-3.1-8B-Instruct`

[16]`commoncrawl.org`

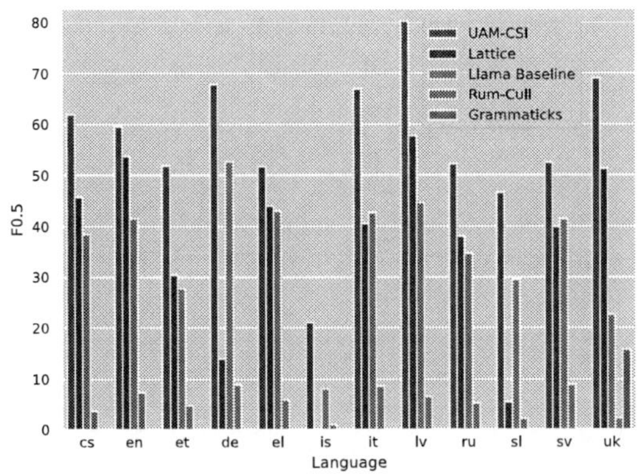

(a) $F_{0.5}$ scores (primary metric) for Track 1 submissions compared with our Llama-based baseline.

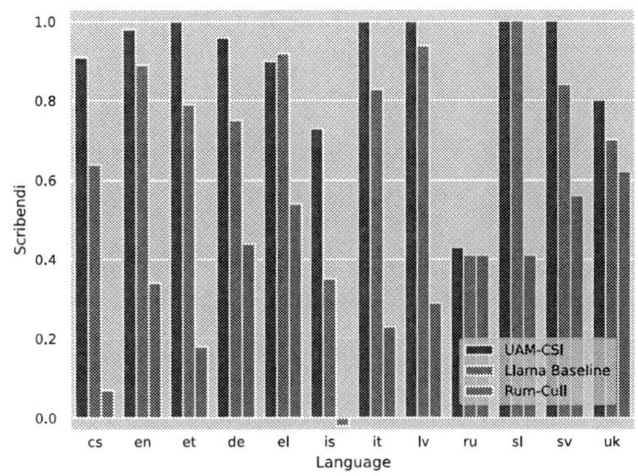

(b) Scribendi scores (primary metric) for Track 2 submissions compared with our Llama-based baseline.

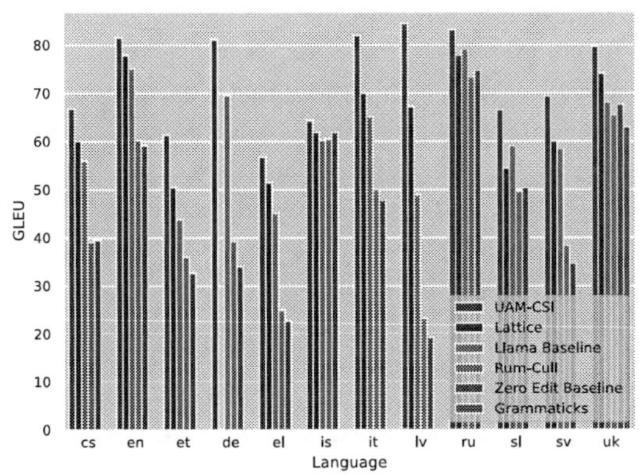

(c) GLEU scores for Track 1 submissions compared with our Llama-based baseline, as well as with a zero-edit baseline.

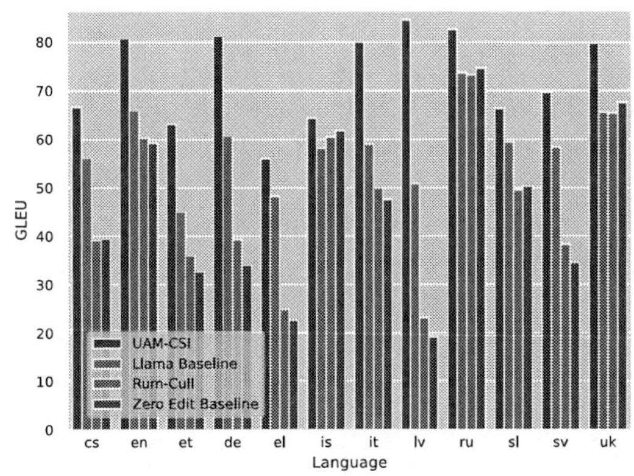

(d) GLEU scores for Track 2 submissions compared with our Llama-based baseline, as well as with a zero-edit baseline.

Figure 3: Overview of the language-wise cross-subcorpus average scores obtained by the submitted systems for different tracks and evaluation metrics. These plots are also available in full size as part of Appendix A.

ures 3c and 3d), since $F_{0.5}$ and Scribendi scores would by definition always be equal to 0.

3 Teams, Approaches and Results

The competitive phase of the shared task ended with four submitting teams. When it comes to the "minimal edits" track (Track 1), three of them – Lattice, Rum-Cull and UAM-CSI – submitted multilingual systems addressing the GEC task for all twelve MultiGEC languages. In addition, a fourth team, Grammaticks, submitted a monolingual system for Ukrainian. Contrary to our expectations, the fluency track (Track 2) was less popular among participants and only received two submissions. Team Rum-Cull submitted the same system output to both tracks, whereas UAM-CSI used two different variants of the same systems for the two tracks.

For both tracks, the winning team is UAM-CSI. Their system, described in Staruch (2025), is the result of fine-tuning the open source LLM Gemma 2. Interestingly – but not decisively in terms of the final ranking, cf. Section 3.2 – this is the same model we selected for the Scribendi-based evaluation. The difference between the two version of this model submitted to the two tracks lies in the amount of data used for fine-tuning: for minimal edits (Track 1), only one reference file per dataset was used, whereas fluency-edited texts (Track 2) were obtained with a system fine-tuned on all available references.

Another team, Lattice, followed a similar approach for the vast majority of the languages, fine-tuning a LLaMA 3 model on MultiGEC data. The team, however, also developed an XLM-RoBERTa-based detection-correction pipeline, which they used for Slovene given LlaMA's low performance on texts in this particular language. Both systems are described in Seminck et al. (2025).

At the time of writing, implementation details for the remaining submissions are not known to the organizers.

3.1 Automatic evaluation

As can be seen in Figure 3, team UAM-CSI is the undisputed winner of the shared task across tracks, languages and evaluation metrics, with only a handful of subcorpus-metric combinations where it is slightly outperformed by the baseline in the fluency track (cf. Appendix C).[17]

In general, our Llama-based one-shot baseline proved hard to beat. When it comes to Track 1, the winning model is the only one consistently outperforming the baseline, with the second-best system beating the latter for ten out of twelve languages in terms of GLEU scores (cf. Figure 3c) and only seven when it comes to $F_{0.5}$, the winning metric (cf. Figure 3a). As for Track 2, the UAM-CSI system scores highest in the vast majority of cases, closely followed and occasionally surpassed by the baseline (cf. Figures 3b and 3d).

Some languages appear to be especially challenging for all of the systems. In particular, all scores are exceptionally low for Icelandic, with only the winning system outperforming a zero-edit baseline in terms of GLEU (cf. Figures 3c-3d) and even a negative Scribendi score (cf. Figure 3b). At the time of writing, we did not have the opportunity to manually assess the quality of any system output for this particular language. However, we can speculate that the small size of the Icelandic subcorpora, especially when it comes to their development and test splits, results in lower scores. Furthermore, the fact that Icelandic is the only language for which only fluency edits are available might also affect the results. Finally, at least for LLM-based systems, poorer performance on this language might be due to limited exposure to the language during pre-training[18]. Russian might also suffer from the latter problem, while the surprisingly low scores that the second-best team, Lattice, obtained on German are to be attributed to the submitted system output being incomplete.

3.2 Preliminary manual evaluation

To provide more insight into the results, we performed a preliminary manual evaluation. This was done systematically on five languages, namely English, German, Italian, Russian and Swedish. While the choice of languages was mostly based on the language skills of the authors of this paper, we argue that it is also representative in a variety of senses. First of all, this selection covers all three language families represented in the dataset, Germanic (English, German and Swedish), Romance (Italian) and Slavic (Russian). Moreover, it includes a language for which several systems scored relatively high (English) one of the more challenging ones (Russian) as well as one for which we observe significant differences between teams (Italian). For each language, we selected one "challenging" case, i.e. a text whose original version greatly differs from the gold reference(s).[19]

Upon manual evaluation, both submissions by the winning team, UAM-CSI, perform generally well, especially for the three Germanic languages considered. In the vast majority of cases, the minimal correction system proposes appropriate changes, but it has a slight tendency towards under-correction. The fluency-oriented system works better overall, but sometimes leads to overcorrection (e.g. for Italian). Yet, some of the more challenging issues, such as those regarding idiomatic expressions and word choice, are occasionally missed, and the system's interpretation of ambiguous or otherwise unclear sentences sometimes differs from that of the human annotators.

Team Lattice only submitted for the minimal track, where it ranked second. To the eyes of the human evaluators, the corrections proposed are reasonable on the whole, although the system occasionally introduces unnecessary or incorrect edits, such as changing plural forms to singular in Swedish and German. Furthermore, despite being submitted to the minimal track, the system

[17]Tables with the complete evaluation results for the two tracks can be found in Appendices B and C. In addition, we provide development-set results as of January 2025 (cf. Appendices D-E).

[18]Details on the exact composition of pre-training data for LLMs on a per-language basis are rarely available, including for the LLMs referred to in this paper.

[19]The manual evaluation is based on six texts with the following essay identifiers: `essay_254e63323678f4d1` (English), `1325_9000532` (Italian), `1023_0101844` and `1031_0003156` (German; in this case, two different essays were used because of the limited submission texts from team Lattice), `FL_IM_authorID-5_essayID-339_test-167` (Russian) and `G34GT1` (Swedish).

sometimes applies fluency edits (this is the case, for instance, in Italian). For Russian, on the other hand, the main issue is under-correction: the system misses over 80% of the errors that were corrected in the human reference text, mostly concerning gender and number agreement in nouns, prepositional phrases and idiomatic expressions.

Team Rum-Cull submitted the same correction hypotheses to both tracks. Across all checked languages, their system consistently applied very few changes, consisting solely of single-word replacements that often fit into the immediate context, but disregard the broader context or alter the meaning of the text. While some of the edits, especially those dealing with spelling and inflection errors, are valid, many introduce drastic semantic changes or lead to further grammaticality issues. As such, the system is currently too unreliable for end-user applications.

Overall, manual inspection confirms the viability of the evaluation metrics discussed in Section 2.2, including those that required adaptation to the highly multilingual scope of the shared task. Given the very small scale of this preliminary evaluation, it is not possible to say whether the scores are cross-lingually consistent: some of the Scribendi scores, for instance, appear suspiciously high. However, the impression we get after examining this sample of the system output is that submissions were ranked fairly. Moreover, the overall low scores for Russian correlate with our empirical observations.

Finally, in an attempt to at least partly explain the low scores registered for all systems on Icelandic data, we glanced at the relevant submissions. Without going into the merits of individual corrections, which would require more expertise in Icelandic, we notice some general trends. First of all, the top-ranking systems, i.e. the UAM-CSI submissions for the two tracks, apply very few corrections. This, however, may simply due to the fact that the texts do not require much editing, which is not unlikely given that one of the two Icelandic subcorpora consists of texts written by native speakers and the other one includes full Master's-level theses, presumably written by highly proficient L2 speakers of the language. Team Rum-Cull's submission, on the other hand, contains many single-word edits, probably overcorrecting the texts. This would explain the negative Scribendi score the team obtained for Icelandic. Finally, team Lattice's submission leaves original texts completely unchanged, thus explaining the $F_{0.5}$ score of 0.

4 Reflections and Takeaways

As mentioned, four teams submitted during the competitive phase of the shared task. Although this number was sufficient to create some competition, it was a pity that several other groups who expressed interest in participating in the task during the development phase did not eventually make any submissions on the test data. In particular, the contrast between the number of submissions and the amount of requests to access the MultiGEC dataset (approximately forty during the competitive phase of the task, increasing to fifty at the time of writing) and CodaLab registrations (twenty during the competitive phase of the task) is striking.

These numbers are evidence as to the rather strong interest in multilingual GEC, whereas the attenuation in active participation is arguably a symptom of the many demands on researchers' time and of the difficulty in developing systems for shared tasks with strict time constraints. Moreover, the task guidelines explicitly prohibited entering the data into commercial LLMs which might also have had an influence. In the following, we reflect on the issues we encountered in our role as shared task organizers and suggest ways to address them in future initiatives.

Timeline The most obvious concern is the timeline. We published our first call for participation in June 2024, a second one in September, and then released the training and development data on 21 October. This gave just over three weeks for system development and tuning until the test phase opened on 13 November. The test phase ran through to 29 November, giving participants just over a fortnight for preparing final submissions. This was an evidently tight timeline, and may have led to some teams failing to make it in time for the test phase. For comparison, the BEA 2019 shared task on GEC (Bryant et al., 2019) involved a development phase of approximately two months, followed by a test phase of just four days. Similarly, MultiGED-2023 (Volodina et al., 2023) had a 1.5-month development phase and one-week test phase. Future competitions should perhaps follow a similar approach.

Evaluation Metrics Evaluating GEC systems is not a straightforward task, with many different existing metrics and implementations to choose from (Bryant et al., 2023). It was desirable that our evaluation method should be well-grounded in the literature and previous shared tasks while being specific and suited to the datasets and languages at hand. In the case of the present shared task, we had two separate tracks calling for different evaluation strategies, data from twelve different languages, and the novelty of dealing with full texts. This introduced an array of additional constraints, which we attempted to satisfy by providing a first adaptation of three existing evaluation metrics, discussed in Section 2.2. This, however, was a time consuming process that resulted in us only disclosing the details of the evaluation procedure upon opening the competitive phase. All in all, our effort can be seen as a first step towards a cross-lingual GEC evaluation framework supporting system that work at the text level.

Benchmarking Platforms An additional layer of complexity comes from the need to fully automate the evaluation process. While this is highly desirable during the competitive phase of a shared task, where any delays affect participants, it becomes essential in cases where the competition is followed by an open phase in which system developers can participate in the task for an indefinite amount of time. Our platform of choice for this shared task, CodaLab, only fulfills this requirement for one of the metric, GLEU. On such platform, it was not possible to set up ERRANT-based or Scribendi scoring due to, respectively, installation issues and resource constraints. More generally, LLM-based evaluation poses particular challenges due to the computational resources involved. In view of future initiatives, but also to ensure that the MultiGEC dataset remains usable, we plan to investigate the available alternatives and potentially migrate the open phase of the shared task to a new platform. Furthermore, we strongly advise organizers of similar events to carefully consider the trade-off between more advanced automatic evaluation metrics and practical viability.

Baseline Since our expectation was for submitted systems to be predominantly LLM-based due to the presence of a fluency track, it was our intention to provide a strong baseline. However, our Llama-based one-shot system proved hard to beat for most of the shared task participants, and it might be the case that this has discouraged submissions of MT-based and other supervised systems, even though it is not necessarily the case that LLM-based systems will outperform supervised ones (Davis et al., 2024).

Data Access One of the main advantages of the dataset compiled for MultiGEC-2025 is that it contains data for all twelve languages in a simple uniform format. Due to licensing issues, however, data access is not entirely straightforward: while most of the training and development data can be obtained from a single repository upon agreeing to the Terms of Use, the English and Russian subcorpora require an additional sign-up and a separate download. Even more importantly, participants do not have direct access to correction hypotheses for the test splits. The reason for this is that some of the data holders of subcorpora that are not in the public domain wish to keep them private. This is a valid standpoint, as having unrestricted access to test data gives system developers the possibility to optimize for it. Moreover, by making test set references public, it can no longer be guaranteed that LLMs have not been exposed to them during pre-training. However, this does pose a problem, especially in conjunction with the evaluation issues mentioned above: participants cannot independently compute reference-based metrics on the test set and there is currently no platform able to fully automate the process. For this reason, we follow a convention emerged from previous shared tasks where data was subject to similar constraints (cf. Bryant et al. (2019)), i.e. to also report results on development data (see Appendices D and E).

5 Conclusions & Future Work

In this paper, we have provided an overview of the MultiGEC-2025 shared task. To the best of our knowledge, this is the first ever shared task on multilingual text-level GEC. We worked with twelve European languages, represented by seventeen subcorpora of texts from a variety of domains, from L2 essays to web news. These were compiled into a single dataset, MultiGEC, which provides all data in an easy-to-use uniform format. The shared task offered two tracks so that participants could choose between two different correction styles: minimal editing, the aim of which is to address grammaticality issues, or fluency editing, where the additional aim is improved idiomaticity.

Having to evaluate submissions in both styles, we opted to use three different evaluation metrics (GLEU, ERRANT scoring, and the Scribendi score) which would either reward faithfulness to the reference corrections or fluency according to a language model. Evaluation was one of the major challenges in the organization of the shared task as these metrics required adaptations to be used in this new, highly multilingual scenario. Our preliminary manual evaluation of a small sample of the results, however, suggests that our solution led to a fair ranking of the submitted systems.

Moreover, we had to deal with the technical limitations of our platform of choice, CodaLab, in terms of automation. Competitors submitted via CodaLab, but only got immediate feedback in the form of GLEU score, while the rest of the evaluation was carried out offline by the organizers. Participants in the ongoing open-phase of the shared task may still submit their corrections to CodaLab to obtain GLEU scores. In addition, we provide a program for automatic GLEU and ERRANT scoring, as well as instructions for setting up Scribendi-based evaluation locally.

Four teams participated in the official competitive phase of the shared task, and the clear winner was the UAM-CSI team with a fine-tuned Gemma 2 model for both tracks. For the most part, this model significantly outperformed our baseline. Our system proved otherwise hard to beat, especially in the 'fluency edits' track (Track 2). Moreover, scores for Icelandic and Russian were generally lower than for the other languages, which may be due to lack of exposure to these languages for LLMs during pre-training, as well as to the peculiarities of the relevant subcorpora.

We dedicated Section 4 to some reflections on the organization of this shared task. These offer insights which can be relevant for planning similar initiatives in future. The high attrition rate in participation that we observed, for instance, could be mitigated by a different timeline, increased data accessibility and further automation of the evaluation routines. While changes to the timeline are in principle easy to implement, the ease of access to the data is, in cases like ours, strongly dependent on the licensing conditions of each source corpus, something to take into account when deciding whether to prioritize the number of languages covered or the usability of the resulting resources. The technicalities of evaluation constitute an even more complex problem, calling for both further work on benchmarking platforms and in terms of development of more lightweight cross-lingually applicable metrics.

Besides these practical aspects, evaluation can be further refined. Language-specific adaptations of ERRANT would enable analysis of system performance by error type and comparisons with state-of-the-art systems could help assess where the multilingual models submitted to MultiGEC-2025 stand with respect to their language-specific counterparts. Moreover, more extensive human evaluation – which we plan to carry out for all twelve languages – would allow us to more profoundly analyze and understand the differences between systems and their continuing weaknesses, and proceed to identify ways to make further improvements to multilingual GEC.

Finally, data-wise, possible directions for future work include collecting additional data and annotations for the current MultiGEC languages so as to make the corpus more balanced and improve the robustness of reference-based evaluation, but also incorporating additional subcorpora into the MultiGEC dataset. New subcorpora could relate to L1 or L2 speakers, different age groups and a variety of genres. We would especially welcome data for languages other than the ones featuring in MultiGEC-2025, including non-European languages, and therefore would welcome contact from those with access to such datasets or planning to collect them.

All in all, despite a limited number of submissions, the shared task resulted in a new highly multilingual resource – the MultiGEC dataset, a promising novel evaluation framework for two variants of the task of GEC and at least one system with a consistently good performance across languages. The amount of requests for data access – about fifty at the time of writing – and CodaLab registrations – twenty during the competitive phase – suggest that interest in the topic is not limited to the shared task itself and encourages us to expand and improve the dataset and continue our work on automatic and manual evaluation.

Acknowledgments

Participants from Sweden have been supported by Nationella Språkbanken and Huminfra, both funded by the Swedish Research Council (2018-2024, contract 2017-00626; 2022-2024, contract

2021-00176) and their participating partner institutions, as well as the Swedish Research Council grants 2019-04129 and 2022-02909. Andrew Caines has been supported by Cambridge University Press & Assessment.

The evaluation was enabled by the National Academic Infrastructure for Supercomputing in Sweden (NAISS), partially funded by the Swedish Research Council through grant agreement no. 202206725. We thank NAISS for providing computational resources under *Projects 2024/22-21 and 2023/22-1238*. Our thanks also go to Christopher Bryant for discussion around the use of ERRANT cross-linguistically.

References

Hiroki Asano, Tomoya Mizumoto, and Kentaro Inui. 2017. Reference-based metrics can be replaced with reference-less metrics in evaluating grammatical error correction systems. In *Proceedings of the Eighth International Joint Conference on Natural Language Processing (Volume 2: Short Papers)*, pages 343–348, Taipei, Taiwan. Asian Federation of Natural Language Processing.

Adriane Boyd. 2018. Using Wikipedia Edits in Low Resource Grammatical Error Correction. In *Proceedings of the 2018 EMNLP Workshop W-NUT: The 4th Workshop on Noisy User-generated Text*, pages 79–84, Brussels, Belgium. Association for Computational Linguistics.

Adriane Boyd, Jirka Hana, Lionel Nicolas, Detmar Meurers, Katrin Wisniewski, Andrea Abel, Karin Schöne, Barbora Štindlová, and Chiara Vettori. 2014. The MERLIN corpus: Learner Language and the CEFR. In *Proceedings of the Ninth International Conference on Language Resources and Evaluation (LREC'14)*, pages 1281–1288, Reykjavik, Iceland. European Language Resources Association (ELRA).

Chris Brockett, William B. Dolan, and Michael Gamon. 2006. Correcting ESL errors using phrasal SMT techniques. In *Proceedings of the 21st International Conference on Computational Linguistics and 44th Annual Meeting of the Association for Computational Linguistics*, pages 249–256, Sydney, Australia. Association for Computational Linguistics.

Christopher Bryant, Mariano Felice, Øistein E. Andersen, and Ted Briscoe. 2019. The BEA-2019 Shared Task on Grammatical Error Correction. In *Proceedings of the Fourteenth Workshop on Innovative Use of NLP for Building Educational Applications*, pages 52–75, Florence, Italy. Association for Computational Linguistics.

Christopher Bryant, Mariano Felice, and Ted Briscoe. 2017. Automatic Annotation and Evaluation of Error Types for Grammatical Error Correction. In *Proceedings of the 55th Annual Meeting of the Association for Computational Linguistics (Volume 1: Long Papers)*, pages 793–805, Vancouver, Canada. Association for Computational Linguistics.

Christopher Bryant, Zheng Yuan, Muhammad Reza Qorib, Hannan Cao, Hwee Tou Ng, and Ted Briscoe. 2023. Grammatical Error Correction: A Survey of the State of the Art. *Computational Linguistics*, pages 643–701.

Leshem Choshen and Omri Abend. 2018. Reference-less measure of faithfulness for grammatical error correction. In *Proceedings of the 2018 Conference of the North American Chapter of the Association for Computational Linguistics: Human Language Technologies, Volume 2 (Short Papers)*, pages 124–129, New Orleans, Louisiana. Association for Computational Linguistics.

Steven Coyne, Keisuke Sakaguchi, Diana Galvan-Sosa, Michael Zock, and Kentaro Inui. 2023. Analyzing the Performance of GPT-3.5 and GPT-4 in Grammatical Error Correction. *arXiv preprint arXiv:2303.14342*.

Roberts Darģis, Ilze Auziņa, Inga Kaija, Kristīne Levāne-Petrova, and Kristīne Pokratniece. 2022. LaVA – Latvian language learner corpus. In *Proceedings of the Thirteenth Language Resources and Evaluation Conference*, pages 727–731, Marseille, France. European Language Resources Association.

Roberts Darģis, Ilze Auziņa, Kristīne Levāne-Petrova, and Inga Kaija. 2020. Quality focused approach to a learner corpus development. In *Proceedings of the Twelfth Language Resources and Evaluation Conference*, pages 392–396, Marseille, France. European Language Resources Association.

Christopher Davis, Andrew Caines, Øistein Andersen, Shiva Taslimipoor, Helen Yannakoudakis, Zheng Yuan, Christopher Bryant, Marek Rei, and Paula Buttery. 2024. Prompting open-source and commercial language models for grammatical error correction of English learner text. In *Findings of the Association for Computational Linguistics: ACL 2024*, pages 11952–11967, Bangkok, Thailand. Association for Computational Linguistics.

Tao Fang, Jinpeng Hu, Derek F. Wong, Xiang Wan, Lidia S. Chao, and Tsung-Hui Chang. 2023. Improving Grammatical Error Correction with Multimodal Feature Integration. In *Findings of the Association for Computational Linguistics: ACL 2023*, pages 9328–9344, Toronto, Canada. Association for Computational Linguistics.

Polona Gantar, Mija Bon, Magdalena Gapsa, and Špela Arhar Holdt. 2023. Šolar-Eval: Evalvacijska množica za strojno popravljanje jezikovnih napak v slovenskih besedilih. *Jezik in slovstvo*, 68(4):89–108.

Aaron Grattafiori, Abhimanyu Dubey, Abhinav Jauhri, Abhinav Pandey, Abhishek Kadian, Ahmad Al-Dahle, Aiesha Letman, Akhil Mathur, Alan Schelten, Alex Vaughan, Amy Yang, Angela Fan, Anirudh Goyal, Anthony Hartshorn, Aobo Yang, Archi Mitra, Archie Sravankumar, Artem Korenev, Arthur Hinsvark, Arun Rao, Aston Zhang, Aurelien Rodriguez, Austen Gregerson, Ava Spataru, Baptiste Roziere, Bethany Biron, Binh Tang, Bobbie Chern, Charlotte Caucheteux, Chaya Nayak, Chloe Bi, Chris Marra, Chris McConnell, Christian Keller, Christophe Touret, Chunyang Wu, Corinne Wong, Cristian Canton Ferrer, Cyrus Nikolaidis, Damien Allonsius, Daniel Song, Danielle Pintz, Danny Livshits, Danny Wyatt, David Esiobu, Dhruv Choudhary, Dhruv Mahajan, Diego Garcia-Olano, Diego Perino, Dieuwke Hupkes, Egor Lakomkin, Ehab AlBadawy, Elina Lobanova, Emily Dinan, Eric Michael Smith, Filip Radenovic, Francisco Guzmán, Frank Zhang, Gabriel Synnaeve, Gabrielle Lee, Georgia Lewis Anderson, Govind Thattai, Graeme Nail, Gregoire Mialon, Guan Pang, Guillem Cucurell, Hailey Nguyen, Hannah Korevaar, Hu Xu, Hugo Touvron, Iliyan Zarov, Imanol Arrieta Ibarra, Isabel Kloumann, Ishan Misra, Ivan Evtimov, Jack Zhang, Jade Copet, Jaewon Lee, Jan Geffert, Jana Vranes, Jason Park, Jay Mahadeokar, Jeet Shah, Jelmer van der Linde, Jennifer Billock, Jenny Hong, Jenya Lee, Jeremy Fu, Jianfeng Chi, Jianyu Huang, Jiawen Liu, Jie Wang, Jiecao Yu, Joanna Bitton, Joe Spisak, Jongsoo Park, Joseph Rocca, Joshua Johnstun, Joshua Saxe, Junteng Jia, Kalyan Vasuden Alwala, Karthik Prasad, Kartikeya Upasani, Kate Plawiak, Ke Li, Kenneth Heafield, Kevin Stone, Khalid El-Arini, Krithika Iyer, Kshitiz Malik, Kuenley Chiu, Kunal Bhalla, Kushal Lakhotia, Lauren Rantala-Yeary, Laurens van der Maaten, Lawrence Chen, Liang Tan, Liz Jenkins, Louis Martin, Lovish Madaan, Lubo Malo, Lukas Blecher, Lukas Landzaat, Luke de Oliveira, Madeline Muzzi, Mahesh Pasupuleti, Mannat Singh, Manohar Paluri, Marcin Kardas, Maria Tsimpoukelli, Mathew Oldham, Mathieu Rita, Maya Pavlova, Melanie Kambadur, Mike Lewis, Min Si, Mitesh Kumar Singh, Mona Hassan, Naman Goyal, Narjes Torabi, Nikolay Bashlykov, Nikolay Bogoychev, Niladri Chatterji, Ning Zhang, Olivier Duchenne, Onur Çelebi, Patrick Alrassy, Pengchuan Zhang, Pengwei Li, Petar Vasic, Peter Weng, Prajjwal Bhargava, Pratik Dubal, Praveen Krishnan, Punit Singh Koura, Puxin Xu, Qing He, Qingxiao Dong, Ragavan Srinivasan, Raj Ganapathy, Ramon Calderer, Ricardo Silveira Cabral, Robert Stojnic, Roberta Raileanu, Rohan Maheswari, Rohit Girdhar, Rohit Patel, Romain Sauvestre, Ronnie Polidoro, Roshan Sumbaly, Ross Taylor, Ruan Silva, Rui Hou, Rui Wang, Saghar Hosseini, Sahana Chennabasappa, Sanjay Singh, Sean Bell, Seohyun Sonia Kim, Sergey Edunov, Shaoliang Nie, Sharan Narang, Sharath Raparthy, Sheng Shen, Shengye Wan, Shruti Bhosale, Shun Zhang, Simon Vandenhende, Soumya Batra, Spencer Whitman, Sten Sootla, Stephane Collot, Suchin Gururangan, Sydney Borodinsky, Tamar Herman, Tara Fowler, Tarek Sheasha, Thomas Georgiou, Thomas Scialom, and Tobias Speckbacher. 2024. The Llama 3 Herd of Models. *arXiv e-prints*, page arXiv:2407.21783.

Anton Karl Ingason, Lilja Björk Stefánsdóttir, Þórunn Arnardóttir, Xindan Xu, Isidora Glišić, and Dagbjört Guðmundsdóttir. 2022. The Icelandic L2 Error Corpus (IceL2EC) 1.3 (22.10). CLARIN-IS.

Anton Karl Ingason, Lilja Björk Stefánsdóttir, Þórunn Arnardóttir, and Xindan Xu. 2021. Icelandic Error Corpus (IceEC) Version 1.1. CLARIN-IS.

Md Asadul Islam and Enrico Magnani. 2021. Is this the end of the gold standard? a straightforward reference-less grammatical error correction metric. In *Proceedings of the 2021 Conference on Empirical Methods in Natural Language Processing*, pages 3009–3015, Online and Punta Cana, Dominican Republic. Association for Computational Linguistics.

Marcin Junczys-Dowmunt and Roman Grundkiewicz. 2014. The AMU system in the CoNLL-2014 shared task: Grammatical error correction by data-intensive and feature-rich statistical machine translation. In *Proceedings of the Eighteenth Conference on Computational Natural Language Learning: Shared Task*, pages 25–33, Baltimore, Maryland. Association for Computational Linguistics.

Katerina Korre, Marita Chatzipanagiotou, and John Pavlopoulos. 2021. ELERRANT: Automatic Grammatical Error Type Classification for Greek. In *Proceedings of the International Conference on Recent Advances in Natural Language Processing (RANLP 2021)*, pages 708–717, Held Online. INCOMA Ltd.

Mengsay Loem, Masahiro Kaneko, Sho Takase, and Naoaki Okazaki. 2023. Exploring Effectiveness of GPT-3 in Grammatical Error Correction: A Study on Performance and Controllability in Prompt-Based Methods. In *Proceedings of the 18th Workshop on Innovative Use of NLP for Building Educational Applications (BEA 2023)*, pages 205–219, Toronto, Canada. Association for Computational Linguistics.

Koki Maeda, Masahiro Kaneko, and Naoaki Okazaki. 2022. IMPARA: Impact-based metric for GEC using parallel data. In *Proceedings of the 29th International Conference on Computational Linguistics*, pages 3578–3588, Gyeongju, Republic of Korea. International Committee on Computational Linguistics.

Arianna Masciolini, Andrew Caines, Orphée De Clercq, Joni Kruijsbergen, Murathan Kurfalı, Ricardo Muñoz Sánchez, Elena Volodina, Robert Östling, Kais Allkivi, Špela Arhar Holdt, Ilze Auzina, Roberts Darģis, Elena Drakonaki, Jennifer-Carmen Frey, Isidora Glišić, Pinelopi Kikilintza, Lionel Nicolas, Mariana Romanyshyn, Alexandr Rosen, Alla Rozovskaya, Kristjan Suluste, Oleksiy Syvokon, Alexandros Tantos,

Despoina-Ourania Touriki, Konstantinos Tsiotskas, Eleni Tsourilla, Vassilis Varsamopoulos, Katrin Wisniewski, Aleš Žagar, and Torsten Zesch. 2025a. Towards better language representation in Natural Language Processing – a multilingual dataset for text-level Grammatical Error Correction. *International Journal of Learner Corpus Research.*

Arianna Masciolini, Andrew Caines, Orphée De Clercq, Joni Kruijsbergen, Murathan Kurfali, Ricardo Muñoz Sánchez, Elena Volodina, Robert Östling, Kais Allkivi-Metsoja, Špela Arhar Holdt, Ilze Auzina, Roberts Darģis, Elena Drakonaki, Jennifer-Carmen Frey, Isidora Glišić, Pinelopi Kikilintza, Lionel Nicolas, Mariana Romanyshyn, Alexandr Rosen, Alla Rozovskaya, Kristjan Suluste, Oleksiy Syvokon, Alexandros Tantos, Despoina-Ourania Touriki, Konstantinos Tsiotskas, Eleni Tsourilla, Vassilis Varsamopoulos, Katrin Wisniewski, Aleš Žagar, and Torsten Zesch. 2025b. MultiGEC [dataset]. Distributed by Språkbanken Text. PID https://doi.org/10.23695/h9f5-8143.

Jakub Náplava, Milan Straka, Jana Straková, and Alexandr Rosen. 2022. Czech Grammar Error Correction with a Large and Diverse Corpus. *Transactions of the Association for Computational Linguistics*, 10:452–467.

Courtney Napoles, Keisuke Sakaguchi, Matt Post, and Joel Tetreault. 2015. Ground Truth for Grammatical Error Correction Metrics. In *Proceedings of the 53rd Annual Meeting of the Association for Computational Linguistics and the 7th International Joint Conference on Natural Language Processing (Volume 2: Short Papers)*, pages 588–593, Beijing, China. Association for Computational Linguistics.

Courtney Napoles, Keisuke Sakaguchi, Matt Post, and Joel Tetreault. 2016a. GLEU without tuning. *arXiv preprint arXiv:1605.02592.*

Courtney Napoles, Keisuke Sakaguchi, and Joel Tetreault. 2016b. There's no comparison: Reference-less evaluation metrics in grammatical error correction. In *Proceedings of the 2016 Conference on Empirical Methods in Natural Language Processing*, pages 2109–2115, Austin, Texas. Association for Computational Linguistics.

Diane Nicholls, Andrew Caines, and Paula Buttery. 2024. The Write & Improve Corpus 2024: Error-annotated and CEFR-labelled essays by learners of English.

Pedro Javier Ortiz Suárez, Benoît Sagot, and Laurent Romary. 2019. Asynchronous pipelines for processing huge corpora on medium to low resource infrastructures. In *Proceedings of the Workshop on Challenges in the Management of Large Corpora (CMLC-7) 2019. Cardiff, 22nd July 2019*, pages 9 – 16, Mannheim. Leibniz-Institut für Deutsche Sprache.

Robert Östling, Katarina Gillholm, Murathan Kurfalı, Marie Mattson, and Mats Wirén. 2024. Evaluation of Really Good Grammatical Error Correction. In *Proceedings of the 2024 Joint International Conference on Computational Linguistics, Language Resources and Evaluation (LREC-COLING 2024)*, pages 6582–6593.

Kishore Papineni, Salim Roukos, Todd Ward, and Wei-Jing Zhu. 2002. Bleu: a Method for Automatic Evaluation of Machine Translation. In *Proceedings of the 40th Annual Meeting of the Association for Computational Linguistics*, pages 311–318, Philadelphia, Pennsylvania, USA. Association for Computational Linguistics.

Alla Rozovskaya and Dan Roth. 2019. Grammar Error Correction in Morphologically Rich Languages: The Case of Russian. *Transactions of the Association for Computational Linguistics*, 7:1–17.

Lisa Rudebeck and Gunlög Sundberg. 2021. SweLL correction annotation guidelines. Technical report, GU-ISS Research report series, Department of Swedish, University of Gothenburg. http://hdl.handle.net/2077/69434.

Olga Seminck, Yoann Dupont, Mathieu Dehouck, Qi Wang, Noé Durandard, and Margo Novikov. 2025. Lattice @MultiGEC-2025: A spitful multilingual language error correction system using LLaMA. In *Proceedings of the 14th Workshop on Natural Language Processing for Computer Assisted Language Learning*, Tallin, Estonia. University of Tartu.

Ryszard Staruch. 2025. UAM-CSI at MultiGEC-2025: Parameter-efficient LLM fine-tuning for multilingual grammatical error correction. In *Proceedings of the 14th Workshop on Natural Language Processing for Computer Assisted Language Learning*, Tallin, Estonia. University of Tartu.

Milan Straka. 2018. UDPipe 2.0 Prototype at CoNLL 2018 UD Shared Task. In *Proceedings of the CoNLL 2018 Shared Task: Multilingual Parsing from Raw Text to Universal Dependencies*, pages 197–207, Brussels, Belgium. Association for Computational Linguistics.

Milan Straka and Jana Straková. 2017. Tokenizing, POS Tagging, Lemmatizing and Parsing UD 2.0 with UDPipe. In *Proceedings of the CoNLL 2017 Shared Task: Multilingual Parsing from Raw Text to Universal Dependencies*, pages 88–99, Vancouver, Canada. Association for Computational Linguistics.

Oleksiy Syvokon, Olena Nahorna, Pavlo Kuchmiichuk, and Nastasiia Osidach. 2023. UA-GEC: Grammatical Error Correction and Fluency Corpus for the Ukrainian Language. In *Proceedings of the Second Ukrainian Natural Language Processing Workshop (UNLP)*, pages 96–102, Dubrovnik, Croatia. Association for Computational Linguistics.

Alexandros Tantos, Nikolaos Amvrazis, and Eleni Drakonaki. 2023. Greek Learner Corpus II (GLCII): Design and development of an online corpus for L2 Greek. *Journal of Applied Linguistics*, 36.

Elena Volodina, Christopher Bryant, Andrew Caines, Orphée De Clercq, Jennifer-Carmen Frey, Elizaveta Ershova, Alexandr Rosen, and Olga Vinogradova. 2023. MultiGED-2023 shared task at NLP4CALL: Multilingual grammatical error detection. In *Proceedings of the 12th Workshop on NLP for Computer Assisted Language Learning*, pages 1–16, Tórshavn, Faroe Islands. LiU Electronic Press.

Elena Volodina, Lena Granstedt, Arild Matsson, Beáta Megyesi, Ildikó Pilán, Julia Prentice, Dan Rosén, Lisa Rudebeck, Carl-Johan Schenström, Gunlög Sundberg, et al. 2019. The SweLL language learner corpus: From design to annotation. *Northern European Journal of Language Technology (NEJLT)*, 6:67–104.

Elena Volodina, Lena Granstedt, Arild Matsson, Beáta Megyesi, Ildikó Pilán, Julia Prentice, Dan Rosén, Lisa Rudebeck, Carl-Johan Schenström, Gunlög Sundberg, and Mats Wirén. 2022. *SweLL-gold [corpus]*. Språkbanken Text. Distributed via SBX/CLARIN.

Katrin Wisniewski, Karin Schöne, Lionel Nicolas, Chiara Vettori, Adriane Boyd, Detmar Meurers, Andrea Abel, and Jirka Hana. 2013. MERLIN: An online trilingual learner corpus empirically grounding the European Reference Levels in authentic learner data. In *International Conference, ICT for Language Learning, 6th Edition*.

Ryoma Yoshimura, Masahiro Kaneko, Tomoyuki Kajiwara, and Mamoru Komachi. 2020. SOME: Reference-less sub-metrics optimized for manual evaluations of grammatical error correction. In *Proceedings of the 28th International Conference on Computational Linguistics*, pages 6516–6522, Barcelona, Spain (Online). International Committee on Computational Linguistics.

Zheng Yuan, Ted Briscoe, and Mariano Felice. 2016. Candidate re-ranking for SMT-based grammatical error correction. In *Proceedings of the 11th Workshop on Innovative Use of NLP for Building Educational Applications*, pages 256–266, San Diego, CA. Association for Computational Linguistics.

A Overview of the official evaluation results

A.1 Track 1 (minimal edits)

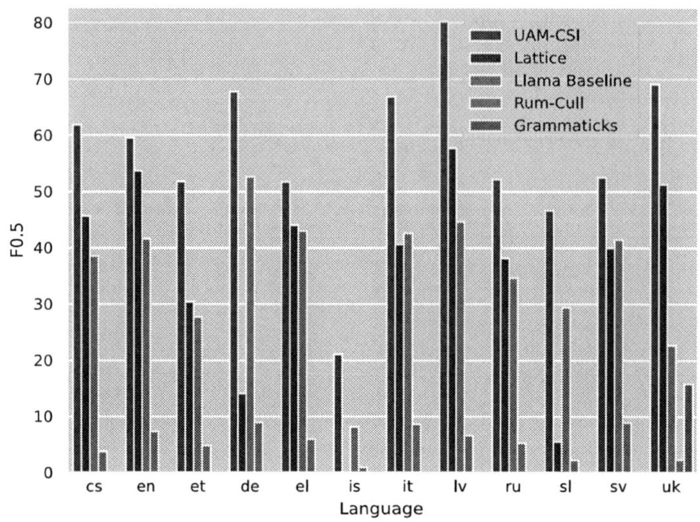

Figure A.1: Language-wise cross-subcorpus average $F_{0.5}$ scores (primary metric) for Track 1 submissions compared with our Llama-based baseline.

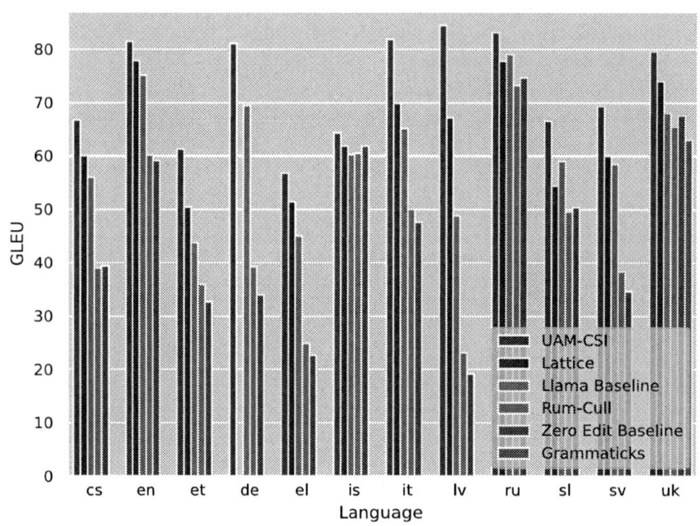

Figure A.2: Language-wise cross-subcorpus average GLEU scores for Track 1 submissions compared with our Llama-based baseline, as well as with a zero-edit baseline.

A.2 Track 2 (fluency edits)

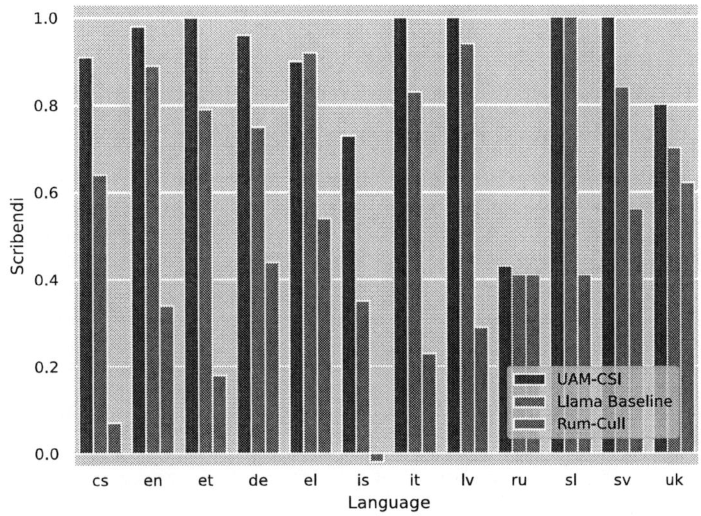

Figure A.3: Language-wise cross-subcorpus average Scribendi scores (primary metric) for Track 2 submissions compared with our Llama-based baseline.

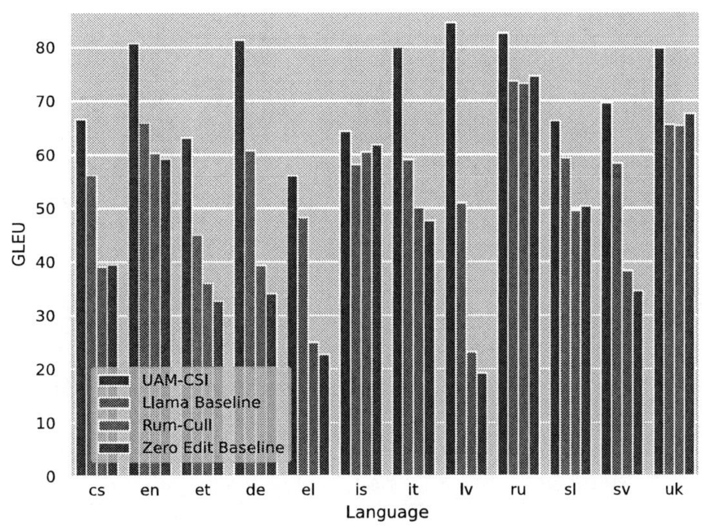

Figure A.4: Language-wise cross-subcorpus average GLEU scores for Track 2 submissions compared with our Llama-based baseline, as well as with a zero-edit baseline.

B Complete official evaluation results for Track 1 (minimal edits)

For this track, systems are ranked based on the ERRANT-based F0.5 score.

B.1 Czech

B.1.1 NatWebInf

Rank	Team	GLEU	Precision	Recall	**F0.5**	Scribendi
1	UAM-CSI	**69.89**	**69.81**	**63.95**	**68.55**	**0.79**
2	Lattice	65.06	56.48	55.29	56.24	0.29
3	baseline	53.91	32.89	33.06	32.93	0.74
4	Rum-Cull	40.47	3.92	1.29	2.78	0.18

B.1.2 Romani

Rank	Team	GLEU	Precision	Recall	**F0.5**	Scribendi
1	UAM-CSI	**60.07**	**59.94**	**50.13**	**57.68**	**0.92**
2	Lattice	53.7	48.52	38.06	45.99	0.84
3	baseline	48.35	38.52	34.52	37.65	0.82
4	Rum-Cull	26.49	6.92	1.34	3.78	0.24

B.1.3 SecLearn

Rank	Team	GLEU	Precision	Recall	**F0.5**	Scribendi
1	UAM-CSI	**55.81**	**62.58**	**47.23**	**58.76**	**0.98**
2	Lattice	49.95	51.69	39.26	48.61	0.94
3	baseline	45.77	50.56	34.28	46.18	0.97
4	Rum-Cull	21.92	11.17	2.77	6.96	0.34

B.1.4 NatForm

Rank	Team	GLEU	Precision	Recall	**F0.5**	Scribendi
1	UAM-CSI	**81.44**	**68.32**	**46.94**	**62.62**	**0.99**
2	baseline	76.08	40.41	29.0	37.46	0.92
3	Lattice	71.45	32.43	30.34	31.99	0.55
4	Rum-Cull	67.18	1.82	1.16	1.63	-0.46

B.1.5 Cross-subcorpus average

Rank	Team	GLEU	Precision	Recall	**F0.5**	Scribendi
1	UAM-CSI	**66.8**	**65.16**	**52.06**	**61.9**	**0.92**
2	Lattice	60.04	47.28	40.74	45.71	0.65
3	baseline	56.03	40.59	32.72	38.55	0.86
4	Rum-Cull	39.02	5.96	1.64	3.79	0.07

B.2 English

B.2.1 Write & Improve 2024

Rank	Team	GLEU	Precision	Recall	**F0.5**	Scribendi
1	UAM-CSI	**81.5**	**62.24**	**50.78**	**59.55**	**0.98**
2	Lattice	77.9	58.05	41.6	53.79	0.95
3	baseline	75.15	41.59	41.55	41.58	**0.98**
4	Rum-Cull	60.2	9.63	3.8	7.37	0.34

B.3 Estonian

B.3.1 EIC

Rank	Team	GLEU	Precision	Recall	**F0.5**	Scribendi
1	UAM-CSI	**55.76**	**54.39**	**36.23**	**49.44**	**1.0**
2	baseline	36.47	34.02	11.42	24.38	0.92
3	Lattice	44.02	22.63	23.18	22.73	0.46
4	Rum-Cull	29.06	6.83	2.06	4.66	-0.04

B.3.2 EKIL2

Rank	Team	GLEU	Precision	Recall	**F0.5**	Scribendi
1	UAM-CSI	**66.85**	**58.82**	**41.28**	**54.21**	**1.0**
2	Lattice	56.96	43.54	25.34	38.07	0.87
3	baseline	51.12	38.73	17.44	31.13	0.97
4	Rum-Cull	42.82	7.47	2.16	5.0	0.4

B.3.3 Cross-subcorpus average

Rank	Team	GLEU	Precision	Recall	**F0.5**	Scribendi
1	UAM-CSI	**61.3**	**56.61**	**38.76**	**51.83**	**1.0**
2	Lattice	50.49	33.09	24.26	30.4	0.66
3	baseline	43.79	36.38	14.43	27.76	0.95
4	Rum-Cull	35.94	7.15	2.11	4.83	0.18

B.4 German

B.4.1 Merlin

Rank	Team	GLEU	Precision	Recall	**F0.5**	Scribendi
1	UAM-CSI	**81.13**	**68.17**	**66.43**	**67.81**	**1.0**
2	baseline	69.56	53.01	51.42	52.68	0.94
3	Lattice	0.05	30.29	4.49	14.09	-0.83
4	Rum-Cull	39.25	12.18	4.34	8.95	0.44

B.5 Greek

B.5.1 GLCII

Rank	Team	GLEU	Precision	Recall	**F0.5**	Scribendi
1	UAM-CSI	**56.84**	**53.79**	**45.11**	**51.8**	**0.88**
2	Lattice	51.49	45.78	38.35	44.07	0.83
3	baseline	45.07	46.95	32.39	43.07	0.97
4	Rum-Cull	24.92	12.53	1.95	6.0	0.54

B.6 Icelandic

B.6.1 IceEC

Rank	Team	GLEU	Precision	Recall	**F0.5**	Scribendi
1	UAM-CSI	**84.98**	**57.28**	**8.45**	**26.58**	**1.0**
2	baseline	80.52	9.6	5.16	8.19	0.67
3	Rum-Cull	81.18	0.85	0.43	0.71	0.22
4	Lattice	83.92	100.0	0.0	0.0	0.0

B.6.2 IceL2EC

Rank	Team	GLEU	Precision	Recall	**F0.5**	Scribendi
1	UAM-CSI	**43.6**	**38.68**	**4.62**	**15.62**	**0.63**
2	baseline	39.93	16.88	2.65	8.14	0.26
3	Rum-Cull	39.77	2.77	0.39	1.25	-0.26
4	Lattice	39.79	100.0	0.0	0.0	0.0

B.6.3 Cross-subcorpus average

Rank	Team	GLEU	Precision	Recall	**F0.5**	Scribendi
1	UAM-CSI	**64.29**	47.98	**6.54**	**21.1**	**0.82**
2	baseline	60.22	13.24	3.91	8.16	0.46
3	Rum-Cull	60.47	1.81	0.41	0.98	-0.02
4	Lattice	61.86	**100.0**	0.0	0.0	0.0

B.7 Italian

B.7.1 Merlin

Rank	Team	GLEU	Precision	Recall	**F0.5**	Scribendi
1	UAM-CSI	**81.89**	**69.04**	**59.54**	**66.91**	**0.98**
2	baseline	65.13	44.01	37.92	42.64	0.8
3	Lattice	69.96	39.9	43.65	40.59	0.85
4	Rum-Cull	50.04	11.13	4.5	8.6	0.23

B.8 Latvian

B.8.1 LaVA

Rank	Team	GLEU	Precision	Recall	**F0.5**	Scribendi
1	UAM-CSI	**84.5**	**80.77**	**78.32**	**80.27**	**1.0**
2	Lattice	67.25	57.8	57.61	57.77	0.9
3	baseline	48.86	47.43	36.32	44.69	**1.0**
4	Rum-Cull	23.18	10.23	2.72	6.59	0.29

B.9 Russian

B.9.1 RULEC-GEC

Rank	Team	GLEU	Precision	Recall	**F0.5**	Scribendi
1	UAM-CSI	**83.11**	**61.09**	33.01	**52.21**	**0.46**
2	Lattice	77.77	42.33	27.38	38.16	0.33
3	baseline	79.02	34.53	**35.46**	34.71	0.42
4	Rum-Cull	73.23	6.34	3.22	5.31	0.41

B.10 Slovene

B.10.1 Solar-Eval

Rank	Team	GLEU	Precision	Recall	**F0.5**	Scribendi
1	UAM-CSI	**66.46**	**53.89**	**30.4**	**46.68**	**1.0**
2	baseline	58.96	35.97	17.06	29.45	0.71
3	Lattice	54.34	8.67	2.25	5.52	-0.06
4	Rum-Cull	49.52	3.64	0.93	2.3	0.59

B.11 Swedish

B.11.1 SweLL_gold

Rank	Team	GLEU	Precision	Recall	**F0.5**	Scribendi
1	UAM-CSI	**69.29**	**54.54**	**45.88**	**52.56**	**1.0**
2	baseline	58.4	44.9	31.74	41.46	**1.0**
3	Lattice	59.88	41.49	35.02	40.01	**1.0**
4	Rum-Cull	38.28	14.02	3.6	8.88	0.56

B.12 Ukrainian

B.12.1 UA-GEC

Rank	Team	GLEU	Precision	Recall	**F0.5**	Scribendi
1	UAM-CSI	**79.55**	**74.31**	**54.11**	**69.15**	**0.89**
2	Lattice	74.0	58.55	34.28	51.29	0.1
3	baseline	68.03	26.1	14.82	22.66	0.41
4	Grammaticks	62.93	16.53	13.48	15.81	-0.1
5	Rum-Cull	65.38	3.15	1.18	2.36	0.62

C Complete official evaluation results for Track 2 (fluency edits)

For this track, systems are ranked based on the Scribendi score.

C.1 Czech

C.1.1 NatWebInf

Rank	Team	GLEU	Precision	Recall	F0.5	**Scribendi**
1	UAM-CSI	**70.04**	**71.05**	**64.28**	**69.58**	**0.79**
2	baseline	51.59	28.32	34.97	29.44	0.25
3	Rum-Cull	40.47	3.92	1.29	2.78	0.18

C.1.2 Romani

Rank	Team	GLEU	Precision	Recall	F0.5	**Scribendi**
1	UAM-CSI	**60.23**	**59.23**	**50.18**	**57.17**	**0.91**
2	baseline	48.55	33.4	33.82	33.48	0.57
3	Rum-Cull	26.49	6.92	1.34	3.78	0.24

C.1.3 SecLearn

Rank	Team	GLEU	Precision	Recall	F0.5	**Scribendi**
1	UAM-CSI	**55.16**	**62.21**	**46.5**	**58.27**	**0.99**
2	baseline	47.7	45.08	36.54	43.07	0.92
3	Rum-Cull	21.92	11.17	2.77	6.96	0.34

C.1.4 NatForm

Rank	Team	GLEU	Precision	Recall	F0.5	**Scribendi**
1	UAM-CSI	**81.07**	**68.71**	**46.82**	**62.83**	**0.95**
2	baseline	76.63	35.45	33.39	35.02	0.82
3	Rum-Cull	67.18	1.82	1.16	1.63	-0.46

C.1.5 Cross-subcorpus average

Rank	Team	GLEU	Precision	Recall	F0.5	**Scribendi**
1	UAM-CSI	**66.63**	**65.3**	**51.95**	**61.96**	**0.91**
2	baseline	56.12	35.56	34.68	35.25	0.64
3	Rum-Cull	39.02	5.96	1.64	3.79	0.07

C.2 English

C.2.1 Write & Improve 2024

Rank	Team	GLEU	Precision	Recall	F0.5	**Scribendi**
1	UAM-CSI	**80.67**	**62.57**	**48.67**	**59.19**	**0.98**
2	baseline	65.86	24.55	40.85	26.68	0.89
3	Rum-Cull	60.2	9.63	3.8	7.37	0.34

C.3 Estonian

C.3.1 EIC

Rank	Team	GLEU	Precision	Recall	F0.5	**Scribendi**
1	UAM-CSI	**57.89**	**56.79**	**38.6**	**51.9**	**1.0**
2	baseline	39.14	31.88	15.6	26.38	0.77
3	Rum-Cull	29.06	6.83	2.06	4.66	-0.04

C.3.2 EKIL2

Rank	Team	GLEU	Precision	Recall	F0.5	**Scribendi**
1	UAM-CSI	**68.23**	**56.66**	**42.86**	**53.23**	**1.0**
2	baseline	50.64	30.57	20.42	27.8	0.81
3	Rum-Cull	42.82	7.47	2.16	5.0	0.4

C.3.3 Cross-subcorpus average

Rank	Team	GLEU	Precision	Recall	F0.5	**Scribendi**
1	UAM-CSI	**63.06**	**56.72**	**40.73**	**52.56**	**1.0**
2	baseline	44.89	31.23	18.01	27.09	0.79
3	Rum-Cull	35.94	7.15	2.11	4.83	0.18

C.4 German

C.4.1 Merlin

Rank	Team	GLEU	Precision	Recall	F0.5	**Scribendi**
1	UAM-CSI	**81.23**	**67.42**	**66.28**	**67.19**	**0.96**
2	baseline	60.67	44.32	50.6	45.45	0.75
3	Rum-Cull	39.25	12.18	4.34	8.95	0.44

C.5 Greek

C.5.1 GLCII

Rank	Team	GLEU	Precision	Recall	F0.5	**Scribendi**
1	baseline	48.27	44.76	35.1	42.43	**0.92**
2	UAM-CSI	**55.96**	**53.62**	**44.12**	**51.4**	0.9
3	Rum-Cull	24.92	12.53	1.95	6.0	0.54

C.6 Icelandic

C.6.1 IceEC

Rank	Team	GLEU	Precision	Recall	F0.5	**Scribendi**
1	UAM-CSI	**85.09**	**61.76**	**9.03**	**28.48**	**0.72**
2	baseline	76.16	10.44	8.88	10.08	0.33
3	Rum-Cull	81.18	0.85	0.43	0.71	0.22

C.6.2 IceL2EC

Rank	Team	GLEU	Precision	Recall	F0.5	**Scribendi**
1	UAM-CSI	**43.62**	**41.18**	4.13	**14.73**	**0.74**
2	baseline	40.08	17.86	**5.01**	11.81	0.37
3	Rum-Cull	39.77	2.77	0.39	1.25	-0.26

C.6.3 Cross-subcorpus average

Rank	Team	GLEU	Precision	Recall	F0.5	**Scribendi**
1	UAM-CSI	**64.36**	**51.47**	**6.58**	**21.61**	**0.73**
2	baseline	58.12	14.15	6.95	10.95	0.35
3	Rum-Cull	60.47	1.81	0.41	0.98	-0.02

C.7 Italian

C.7.1 Merlin

Rank	Team	GLEU	Precision	Recall	F0.5	**Scribendi**
1	UAM-CSI	**79.97**	**67.45**	**56.67**	**64.98**	**1.0**
2	baseline	59.03	32.06	39.89	33.37	0.83
3	Rum-Cull	50.04	11.13	4.5	8.6	0.23

C.8 Latvian

C.8.1 LaVA

Rank	Team	GLEU	Precision	Recall	F0.5	**Scribendi**
1	UAM-CSI	**84.65**	**79.76**	**78.54**	**79.51**	**1.0**
2	baseline	50.92	45.57	38.92	44.07	0.94
3	Rum-Cull	23.18	10.23	2.72	6.59	0.29

C.9 Russian

C.9.1 RULEC-GEC

Rank	Team	GLEU	Precision	Recall	F0.5	**Scribendi**
1	UAM-CSI	**82.65**	**62.3**	30.94	**51.8**	0.43
2	baseline	73.63	24.02	**37.37**	25.87	0.41
3	Rum-Cull	73.23	6.34	3.22	5.31	0.41

C.10 Slovene

C.10.1 Solar-Eval

Rank	Team	GLEU	Precision	Recall	F0.5	**Scribendi**
1	UAM-CSI	**66.32**	**54.14**	**29.77**	**46.52**	**1.0**
2	baseline	59.42	30.84	20.58	28.04	**1.0**
3	Rum-Cull	49.52	3.64	0.93	2.3	0.41

C.11 Swedish

C.11.1 SweLL_gold

Rank	Team	GLEU	Precision	Recall	F0.5	**Scribendi**
1	UAM-CSI	**69.62**	**55.29**	**46.69**	**53.32**	**1.0**
2	baseline	58.41	36.62	34.0	36.06	0.84
3	Rum-Cull	38.28	14.02	3.6	8.88	0.56

C.12 Ukrainian

C.12.1 UA-GEC

Rank	Team	GLEU	Precision	Recall	F0.5	**Scribendi**
1	UAM-CSI	**79.82**	**74.65**	**55.02**	**69.68**	**0.8**
2	baseline	65.56	19.41	18.45	19.21	0.7
3	Rum-Cull	65.38	3.15	1.18	2.36	0.62

D Results on development data for Track 1 (minimal edits) as of January 2025

For this track, systems are ranked based on the ERRANT-based F0.5 score.

D.1 Czech

D.1.1 NatWebInf

Rank	Team	GLEU	Precision	Recall	**F0.5**	Scribendi
1	UAM-CSI	**75.64**	**67.25**	**62.7**	**66.29**	**0.76**
2	Lattice	77.64	49.31	58.35	50.88	-0.55
3	baseline	60.9	33.85	33.75	33.83	0.44

D.1.2 Romani

Rank	Team	GLEU	Precision	Recall	**F0.5**	Scribendi
1	UAM-CSI	**64.71**	**56.88**	**51.64**	**55.75**	**0.92**
2	Lattice	58.02	46.18	43.49	45.62	0.6
3	baseline	55.14	37.14	34.89	36.67	0.83

D.1.3 SecLearn

Rank	Team	GLEU	Precision	Recall	**F0.5**	Scribendi
1	UAM-CSI	**58.33**	**60.66**	**49.67**	**58.09**	**0.99**
2	Lattice	52.63	48.79	41.49	47.13	0.94
3	baseline	46.35	46.76	34.94	43.79	0.97

D.1.4 NatForm

Rank	Team	GLEU	Precision	Recall	**F0.5**	Scribendi
1	UAM-CSI	**84.41**	**63.32**	**49.79**	**60.05**	**0.95**
2	baseline	81.16	44.56	36.32	42.62	0.8
3	Lattice	79.52	40.58	36.14	39.61	-0.02

D.1.5 Cross-subcorpus average

Rank	Team	GLEU	Precision	Recall	**F0.5**	Scribendi
1	UAM-CSI	**70.77**	**62.03**	**53.45**	**60.05**	**0.91**
2	Lattice	66.95	46.21	44.87	45.81	0.24
3	baseline	60.89	40.58	34.98	39.23	0.76

D.2 English

D.2.1 Write & Improve 2024

Rank	Team	GLEU	Precision	Recall	**F0.5**	Scribendi
1	UAM-CSI	**82.6**	**62.62**	**49.86**	**59.57**	**0.99**
2	Lattice	79.44	54.35	40.2	50.78	0.36
3	baseline	76.43	39.25	42.24	39.82	0.98

D.3 Estonian

D.3.1 EIC

Rank	Team	GLEU	Precision	Recall	**F0.5**	Scribendi
1	UAM-CSI	**55.5**	**50.52**	**33.84**	**45.98**	**1.0**
2	Lattice	49.54	32.36	27.51	31.26	0.31
3	baseline	36.01	32.08	10.8	23.01	0.92

D.3.2 EKIL2

Rank	Team	GLEU	Precision	Recall	**F0.5**	Scribendi
1	UAM-CSI	**66.89**	**52.45**	**37.08**	**48.43**	**0.98**
2	Lattice	57.71	36.48	21.86	32.17	0.35
3	baseline	54.48	34.81	15.15	27.64	0.84

D.3.3 Cross-subcorpus average

Rank	Team	GLEU	Precision	Recall	**F0.5**	Scribendi
1	UAM-CSI	**61.19**	**51.48**	**35.46**	**47.2**	**0.99**
2	Lattice	53.63	34.42	24.69	31.71	0.33
3	baseline	45.25	33.45	12.98	25.32	0.88

D.4 German

D.4.1 Merlin

Rank	Team	GLEU	Precision	Recall	**F0.5**	Scribendi
1	UAM-CSI	**80.31**	**67.23**	**63.76**	**66.51**	**0.94**
2	baseline	69.16	51.89	50.55	51.61	0.9
3	Lattice	0.0	31.8	3.35	11.79	-0.92

D.5 Greek

D.5.1 GLCII

Rank	Team	GLEU	Precision	Recall	**F0.5**	Scribendi
1	UAM-CSI	**57.57**	**53.56**	**44.7**	**51.52**	0.84
2	Lattice	54.68	48.47	40.17	46.55	0.74
3	baseline	47.68	49.83	33.17	45.29	**0.9**

D.6 Icelandic

D.6.1 IceEC

Rank	Team	GLEU	Precision	Recall	**F0.5**	Scribendi
1	UAM-CSI	**88.62**	**34.57**	6.53	**18.59**	**0.5**
2	baseline	85.3	9.84	**7.23**	9.18	0.22
3	Lattice	0.88	0.0	0.0	0.0	-1.0

D.6.2 IceL2EC

Rank	Team	GLEU	Precision	Recall	**F0.5**	Scribendi
1	baseline	45.05	**26.78**	**6.18**	**16.06**	0.16
2	UAM-CSI	**48.19**	22.87	3.99	11.75	**0.89**
3	Lattice	2.52	0.4	1.25	0.46	-0.89

D.6.3 Cross-subcorpus average

Rank	Team	GLEU	Precision	Recall	**F0.5**	Scribendi
1	UAM-CSI	**68.4**	**28.72**	5.26	**15.17**	**0.7**
2	baseline	65.17	18.31	**6.71**	12.62	0.19
3	Lattice	1.7	0.2	0.62	0.23	-0.95

D.7 Italian

D.7.1 Merlin

Rank	Team	GLEU	Precision	Recall	**F0.5**	Scribendi
1	UAM-CSI	**80.27**	**68.3**	**60.9**	**66.68**	**0.98**
2	Lattice	77.15	53.78	58.11	54.6	0.58
3	baseline	66.5	50.66	43.83	49.13	0.85

D.8 Latvian

D.8.1 LaVA

Rank	Team	GLEU	Precision	Recall	**F0.5**	Scribendi
1	UAM-CSI	**83.89**	**81.32**	**78.62**	**80.76**	**1.0**
2	Lattice	69.09	61.73	61.33	61.65	0.94
3	baseline	47.3	48.44	38.14	45.96	0.98

D.9 Russian

D.9.1 RULEC-GEC

Rank	Team	GLEU	Precision	Recall	**F0.5**	Scribendi
1	UAM-CSI	**84.68**	**52.98**	35.63	**48.28**	0.37
2	baseline	77.82	24.84	36.54	26.54	**0.43**
3	Lattice	79.35	21.03	**36.86**	23.01	-0.86

D.10 Slovene

D.10.1 Solar-Eval

Rank	Team	GLEU	Precision	Recall	**F0.5**	Scribendi
1	UAM-CSI	**67.22**	**57.4**	**32.89**	**49.95**	**1.0**
2	baseline	59.55	37.2	18.86	31.14	**1.0**
3	Lattice	29.69	14.17	6.77	11.63	-0.12

D.11 Swedish

D.11.1 SweLL_gold

Rank	Team	GLEU	Precision	Recall	**F0.5**	Scribendi
1	UAM-CSI	**72.01**	**58.83**	**50.61**	**56.98**	**1.0**
2	baseline	56.48	48.46	30.79	43.47	0.92
3	Lattice	59.95	45.02	35.33	42.68	0.88

D.12 Ukrainian

D.12.1 UA-GEC

Rank	Team	GLEU	Precision	Recall	**F0.5**	Scribendi
1	UAM-CSI	**77.62**	**70.34**	**49.31**	**64.81**	**0.9**
2	Lattice	66.01	33.96	27.53	32.45	-0.33
3	baseline	67.29	25.15	16.61	22.81	0.64

E Results on development data for Track 2 (fluency edits) as of January 2025

For this track, systems are ranked based on the Scribendi score.

E.1 Czech

E.1.1 NatWebInf

Rank	Team	GLEU	Precision	Recall	F0.5	**Scribendi**
1	UAM-CSI	**76.34**	**68.68**	**64.25**	**67.74**	**0.76**
2	baseline	56.9	26.37	32.49	27.4	0.39

E.1.2 Romani

Rank	Team	GLEU	Precision	Recall	F0.5	**Scribendi**
1	UAM-CSI	**64.68**	**58.34**	**51.58**	**56.85**	**0.92**
2	baseline	50.87	32.12	33.71	32.43	0.7

E.1.3 SecLearn

Rank	Team	GLEU	Precision	Recall	F0.5	**Scribendi**
1	UAM-CSI	**58.11**	**60.58**	**49.55**	**58.0**	**0.98**
2	baseline	47.01	43.0	36.28	41.46	0.94

E.1.4 NatForm

Rank	Team	GLEU	Precision	Recall	F0.5	**Scribendi**
1	UAM-CSI	**84.55**	**65.47**	**50.7**	**61.86**	**0.95**
2	baseline	78.93	31.78	36.73	32.66	0.89

E.1.5 Cross-subcorpus average

Rank	Team	GLEU	Precision	Recall	F0.5	**Scribendi**
1	UAM-CSI	**70.92**	**63.27**	**54.02**	**61.11**	**0.9**
2	baseline	58.43	33.32	34.8	33.49	0.73

E.2 English

E.2.1 Write & Improve 2024

Rank	Team	GLEU	Precision	Recall	F0.5	**Scribendi**
1	UAM-CSI	**81.98**	**63.68**	**47.61**	**59.65**	**0.98**
2	baseline	66.34	21.76	40.96	24.01	0.91

E.3 Estonian

E.3.1 EKIL2

E.3.2 EIC

Rank	Team	GLEU	Precision	Recall	F0.5	**Scribendi**
1	UAM-CSI	**58.19**	**53.13**	**38.62**	**49.42**	**1.0**
2	baseline	37.04	32.37	14.13	25.73	0.77

Rank	Team	GLEU	Precision	Recall	F0.5	**Scribendi**
1	UAM-CSI	**67.91**	**52.61**	**38.92**	**49.15**	**0.99**
2	baseline	52.5	27.9	17.93	25.11	0.84

E.3.3 Cross-subcorpus average

Rank	Team	GLEU	Precision	Recall	F0.5	**Scribendi**
1	UAM-CSI	**63.05**	**52.87**	**38.77**	**49.28**	**0.99**
2	baseline	44.77	30.13	16.03	25.42	0.8

E.4 German

E.4.1 Merlin

Rank	Team	GLEU	Precision	Recall	F0.5	**Scribendi**
1	UAM-CSI	**81.05**	**67.53**	**64.36**	**66.87**	**0.96**
2	baseline	65.22	43.85	49.66	44.9	0.84

E.5 Greek

E.5.1 GLCII

Rank	Team	GLEU	Precision	Recall	F0.5	**Scribendi**
1	baseline	50.39	47.79	36.09	44.88	**0.91**
2	UAM-CSI	**57.98**	**53.88**	**44.7**	**51.76**	0.84

E.6 Icelandic

E.6.1 IceEC

Rank	Team	GLEU	Precision	Recall	F0.5	**Scribendi**
1	UAM-CSI	**88.29**	**28.12**	4.2	**13.14**	**0.61**
2	baseline	79.56	7.6	**8.62**	7.78	0.33

E.6.2 IceL2EC

Rank	Team	GLEU	Precision	Recall	F0.5	**Scribendi**
1	UAM-CSI	**48.62**	21.28	3.64	10.8	**0.89**
2	baseline	45.71	**22.15**	**8.13**	**16.47**	0.58

E.6.3 Cross-subcorpus average

Rank	Team	GLEU	Precision	Recall	F0.5	**Scribendi**
1	UAM-CSI	**68.46**	**24.7**	3.92	11.97	**0.75**
2	baseline	62.64	14.88	**8.38**	**12.12**	0.46

E.7 Italian

E.7.1 Merlin

Rank	Team	GLEU	Precision	Recall	F0.5	**Scribendi**
1	UAM-CSI	**80.04**	**70.3**	**60.11**	**68.0**	**0.98**
2	baseline	56.85	35.03	41.54	36.16	0.85

E.8 Latvian

E.8.1 LaVA

Rank	Team	GLEU	Precision	Recall	F0.5	**Scribendi**
1	UAM-CSI	**83.32**	**81.29**	**78.95**	**80.81**	**0.98**
2	baseline	47.97	44.89	38.78	43.52	0.94

E.9 Russian

E.9.1 RULEC-GEC

Rank	Team	GLEU	Precision	Recall	F0.5	**Scribendi**
1	baseline	72.64	18.99	**39.04**	21.17	**0.47**
2	UAM-CSI	**83.95**	**53.71**	32.03	**47.3**	0.34

E.10 Slovene

E.10.1 Solar-Eval

Rank	Team	GLEU	Precision	Recall	F0.5	**Scribendi**
1	UAM-CSI	**66.99**	**57.16**	**32.49**	**49.63**	**1.0**
2	baseline	59.84	30.57	22.56	28.54	**1.0**

E.11 Swedish

E.11.1 SweLL_gold

Rank	Team	GLEU	Precision	Recall	F0.5	**Scribendi**
1	UAM-CSI	**70.38**	**57.81**	**48.29**	**55.62**	**1.0**
2	baseline	60.05	39.27	34.7	38.26	1.0

E.12 Ukrainian

E.12.1 UA-GEC

Rank	Team	GLEU	Precision	Recall	F0.5	**Scribendi**
1	UAM-CSI	**77.54**	**69.12**	**50.95**	**64.52**	**0.9**
2	baseline	64.65	18.88	20.66	19.21	0.77

Lattice @MultiGEC-2025: A Spitful Multilingual Language Error Correction System Using LLaMA

Olga Seminck[1], Yoann Dupont[1], Mathieu Dehouck[1], Qi Wang[1], Noé Durandard[1], Margo Novikov[1]

[1]LaTTiCe UMR8094 : CNRS, ENS-PSL, Sorbonne-Nouvelle, Paris, France
olga.seminck@cnrs.fr, yoann.dupont@sorbonne-nouvelle.fr, mathieu.dehouck@cnrs.fr, qi.wang@cnrs.fr, noe.durandard@psl.eu, margosha.novikova@gmail.com

Abstract

This paper reports on our submission to the NLP4CALL shared task on Multilingual Grammatical Error Correction (MultiGEC-2025) (Masciolini et al., 2025). We developed two approaches: fine-tuning a large language model, LLaMA 3.0 (8B), for each MultiGEC corpus, and a pipeline based on the encoder-based language model XLM-RoBERTa. During development, the first method significantly outperformed the second, except for languages that are poorly supported by LLaMA 3.0 and have limited MultiGEC training data. Therefore, our official results for the shared task were produced using the neural network system for Slovenian, while fine-tuned LLaMA models were used for the eleven other languages. In this paper, we first introduce the shared task and its data. Next, we present our two approaches, as well as a method to detect cycles in the LLaMA output. We also discuss a number of hurdles encountered while working on the shared task.

1 Introduction

South American camelids are infamous for spitting at each other and at people's faces. Working on the MultiGEC-2025 shared task on grammatical error correction, we realized that LLaMA 3.0 is no different.

Grammatical Error Correction (GEC) is a fundamental task in Natural Language Processing (NLP) for bureautics and educational settings, aimed at automatically identifying and correcting grammatical errors in written texts. As a helping tool in second language acquisition (Volodina et al., 2023), it is essential for addressing diverse learning needs and backgrounds (Loem et al., 2023) that GEC be able to handle various modes of correction, such as minimal and fluency edits,. Minimal edit correction focuses on addressing grammatical errors while preserving the original form and structure of the text, whereas fluency correction involves rewriting texts to enhance idiomaticity and achieve greater naturalness (Davis et al., 2024). The errors to identify are not limited to grammatical errors; other types such as orthographical, syntactical and lexical errors need also be considered.

Research in GEC has advanced significantly over the past decades, from rule-based methods (Sidorov et al., 2013) to statistical approaches (Yuan and Felice, 2013), followed by neural network models (Bryant et al., 2023), and most recently, large language models (LLMs), such as OpenAI's GPT and Meta's LLaMA LLMs (Davis et al., 2024).

The objective of the NLP4CALL shared task, MultiGEC-2025 (Masciolini et al., 2025), is to perform grammatical error correction (GEC) on 12 languages: Czech, English, Estonian, German, Greek, Icelandic, Italian, Latvian, Russian, Slovene, Swedish, and Ukrainian. The shared task requires rewriting texts produced by language learners to make them either grammatically correct (minimal edits) or both grammatically correct and idiomatic (fluency edits) (Table 1).

In this paper, we present the systems submitted by our team, Lattice, to the MultiGEC-2025 shared task, which was hosted as part of the 14th Workshop on Natural Language Pro-

Olga Seminck, Yoann Dupont, Mathieu Dehouck, Qi Wang, Noé Durandard and Margo Novikov. Lattice @MultiGEC-2025: A Spitful Multilingual Language Error Correction System Using LLaMA. *Proceedings of the 14th Workshop on Natural Language Processing for Computer Assisted Language Learning (NLP4CALL 2025).* University of Tartu Library. 34–41.

cessing for Computer-Assisted Language Learning (NLP4CALL). The structure of this paper is as follows: first, we provide an overview of the dataset introduced by the organizers. Next, we describe the two methods we developed: one based on fine-tuning the LLaMA 3.0 model (Touvron et al., 2023), and the other based on the XLM-RoBERTa language model (Conneau et al., 2020), followed by a method to detect and remove cycles in the LLaMa output that we used to enhance the results. Finally, we present an analysis of our system's results in relation to the particularities of the 17 different corpora included in the shared task's data.

Input	My mother became very sad, no food. But my sister better five months later.
Minimal Correction	My mother became very sad, and ate no food. But my sister felt better five months later.
Fluency Correction	My mother was very distressed and refused to eat. Luckily, my sister recovered five months later.

Table 1: An example of an input text with reference corrections (minimal and fluency edits).

2 Data

Table 2 presents detailed statistics of the corpus, including the number of essays, word counts, and sentence counts, calculated using the syntok tokenizer provided by the MultiGEC organizers. These statistics focus exclusively on the original written essays (i.e., excluding rewritten essays produced by our systems). The data highlights the structural diversity across the datasets, with essay lengths varying significantly depending on the source language of each dataset.

On average, each essay contains 277 tokens. Notably, Icelandic essays are considerably longer, with the IceEC dataset averaging 1,004 tokens per essay and the IceL2EC dataset averaging 818 tokens. Similarly, Slovene essays in the Solar-Eval dataset average 642 tokens per essay. In contrast, the Russian dataset has a significantly lower average, with essays containing only 38 tokens per essay.

Most datasets follow the traditional split of approximately 80% for training, 10% for development, and 10% for testing. However, there are exceptions. The Slovene dataset is relatively small, consisting of only 109 essays. Its splits are notably unbalanced, with 10 essays in the training set, 50 in the development set, and 49 in the test set. In contrast, the Russian dataset is split more evenly, with 42% allocated for training, 33% for development, and 25% for testing.

3 Methods

3.1 Baseline

The MultiGEC organizers offer a one-shot multilingual baseline leveraging the LLaMA 3.1 8B Instruct model. In this approach, a single example in English is incorporated into the prompt, addressing binary scenarios that focus on either minimal edits or fluency edits.

3.2 Fine-tuned LLaMA 3.0 8B

The methodology applied by our team was *peft* (parameter-efficient fine-tuning) with 4-bit NormalFloat quantization using QLora (Dettmers et al., 2024), a method based on *Low-Rank Adaptation* (LoRA) (Biderman et al., 2024), for fine-tuning the LLaMA 8B 3.0 model (Touvron et al., 2023). We choose peft due to its higher efficiency in terms of computational requirements and its ability to prevent model collapse and catastrophic forgetting [1]. We utilized a single RTX 3090 GPU with 24GB of RAM for training and testing. The process consumed approximately 97% of the available memory, indicating that experimenting with a heavier model would likely be infeasible given our current infrastructure.

During the development phase, we observed that fine-tuning a model on each training set and then applying it to the corresponding development set led to improved performance compared to using a single model per language. We thus decided to fine-tune one model per corpus, resulting in 17 models in total. During the test phase, training data consisted of the concatenation of the MultiGEC training and development sets, as we noticed that corpora with more training data tended to achieve higher performance.

During the development phase, we also observed that essays lacking a strong punctuation

[1]https://ai.meta.com/blog/how-to-fine-tune-llms-peft-dataset-curation/

Lang.	Source	Split	#Essays	#Sents.	#Tokens
		train	227	3,245	44,261
Czech	NatForm	dev	88	1,537	22,206
		test	76	1,433	19,962
		train	3,620	6,463	87,345
Czech	NatWebInf	dev	1,291	2,270	31,118
		test	1,256	2,059	26,963
		train	2,057	27,741	331,953
Czech	SecLearn	dev	173	2,608	32,106
		test	177	2,710	35,264
		train	3,247	18,198	280,268
Czech	Romani	dev	179	900	14,616
		test	173	967	15,706
		train	4,040	37,341	680,405
English	Write & Improve	dev	506	4,307	89,132
		test	504	4,911	93,419
		train	206	2,849	33,923
Estonian	EIC	dev	26	366	4,491
		test	26	385	4,344
		train	1,202	14,400	189,162
Estonian	EKIL2	dev	150	1,853	24,546
		test	151	1,676	23,103
		train	827	8,455	117,345
German	Merlin	dev	103	1,102	15,762
		test	103	1,029	13,361
		train	1,031	12,167	207,606
Greek	GLCII	dev	129	1,538	26,385
		test	129	1,525	24,640
		train	140	7,146	141,439
Icelandic	IceEC	dev	18	784	16,028
		test	18	905	19,178
		train	155	5,470	124,750
Icelandic	IceL2EC	dev	19	741	18,899
		test	19	595	14,329
		train	651	6,620	83,419
Italian	Merlin	dev	81	818	10,704
		test	81	845	10,562
		train	813	17,254	148,701
Latvian	LaVA	dev	101	2228	18,514
		test	101	2,091	17,995
		train	2,539	5,191	90,424
Russian	RULEC-GEC	dev	1,969	2,688	45,260
		test	1,535	5,321	92,337
		train	10	253	5,062
Slovene	Solar-Eval	dev	50	1,672	31,365
		test	49	1,775	33,515
		train	402	6,294	120,433
Swedish	SweLL_gold	dev	50	724	13,232
		test	50	653	12,066
		train	1,706	29,429	460,385
Ukrainian	UA-GEC	dev	87	1,318	23,953
		test	79	1,089	20,030

Table 2: MultiGEC data statistics (original files using the syntok tokenizer).

marker at the end often resulted in excessively long outputs. To address this, we added a stop token ("$$$") to the end of each essay. After generation, these stop tokens were removed.

To formalize the roles of the prompt, input, and correct output, we transformed the data into a .json format. The prompt it the same for all 17 corpora and is taken from the original provided baseline: *"You are a grammatical error correction tool. Your task is to correct the grammaticality and spelling of the input essay written by a learner. Return only the corrected text and nothing more."*

The tokens per essay were counted using the LLaMA tokenizer[2]. For each corpus, the maximum number of tokens was used to determine the maximum generation length, which was set to this number plus 15%. For example, for Italian, the maximum token length was 478, so this parameter was set to 550. Keeping this number as low as possible is important because setting it too high significantly slows down the prediction process.

For all languages, we used batches of 10 essays and set the gradient accumulation parameter to 4 steps. The number of optimization steps is provided in Table 3. Initially, we set the number of optimization steps to 500. However, after training about half of the models, we realized that we did not have enough time left before the system submission deadline, so we trained the remaining models with fewer optimization steps.

We did not conduct quantitative research on the relationship between the number of optimization steps and model performance. Therefore, it is possible that similar performance could be achieved with fewer optimization steps or that better performance could be obtained with more optimization steps.

3.2.1 Detection of Cycles in LLaMA's Outputs

Despite using a stop token ("$$$") to help the model interrupt the generation process, the model still occasionally loops and repeats the same sentence (or a few sentences) until it reaches the allotted number of tokens for the current essay.

In order to mitigate this undesired behaviour, we passed the outputs of the LLaMA model to an ad-hoc repetition detector which works as follows: Given a string of characters s_i with i ranging from 0 to l, the length of the string. For each character n-gram r ($n = 15$ in this case), we get the sorted list of indices at which r appears in s. From this list, we compute the distance between each pair of consecutive occurrences of r. Eventually, if there are at least 20 occurrences of r with 10 or more pairs of the same distance, especially toward the end of the essay, we flag the essay.

In theory, a model could recover from a cycle since its internal state evolves during the generation process, and it could also experience very long cycles. However, in practice, detecting 10 or more similarly spaced occurrences of 15 characters at the end of an essay was sufficient for capturing LLaMA's loops.

This tool was used for both diagnosis and intervention. When only a few essays are flagged for loops, we address them with a simple rule. If the loop is a well-formed sentence (i.e., it starts with an uppercase letter and ends with punctuation), we cut the essay after the first occurrence of the loop. If the beginning of the loop can be found in the original essay, we append the end of the original essay to our correction. If the loop is not a well-formed sentence, we cut at the end of the last well-formed sentence before the loop and append the rest of the original essay. This approach helps avoid losing too much of the essay if the loop occurs early in the text.

For example, in the Czech NatForm corpus, out of the 646 essays, two had loops (30 repetitions of 115 characters for one, and 41 repetitions of 42 characters for the other). The 30 repetitions correspond to the sequence *"Na druhém boku je zástrčka na sluchátka. Na vrchu mobilu je zástrčka na nabíjení, USB kabel a tlačítko na vypnutí."* The detected r is actually "*. Na druhém bok*", since it is present in the original essay, we remove the repeating section and replace it with the end of the original essay.

Fined-tuned Llama did not generate looping text on most corpora. The Czech NatWebInf had one problematic essay (out of 1256) due to a long string of dashes "-". There was one problematic essay in the Greek GLCII corpus (out of 481), and one in the Ukrainian UA_GEC corpus (out of 456). However, from the 49 Slovene Solar-Eval essays, 11 were problematic (22.44%) and virtually all Icelandic essays were problematic as well. As a result, we decided to use use the XLM-Roberta detect and correct model (described below) for Slovene and to simply return the original, untouched texts for Icelandic.

[2] Note that this is a different tokenizer from the syntok tokenizer used to count the number of tokens in Table 2. The syntok tokenizer is used to separate words and punctuation symbols in order to compute the various scores of a proposed correction, while LLaMA's tokenizer is used internally by the language model for vectorizing its inputs in order to deal with rare or out of vocabulary words.

Lang.	Source	#Optimization Steps
Czech	NatForm	150
Czech	NatWebInf	500
Czech	SecLearn	200
Czech	Romani	150
English	Write & Improve	200
Estonian	EIC	150
Estonian	EKIL2	150
German	Merlin	500
Greek	GLCII	150
Icelandic	IceEC	500
Icelandic	IceL2EC	500
Italian	Merlin	500
Latvian	LaVA	500
Russian	RULEC-GEC	150
Slovene	Solar-Eval	50
Swedish	SweLL_gold	150
Ukrainian	UA-GEC	200

Table 3: The number of optimization steps per corpus during the fine-tuning of the LLaMA models.

3.3 Detect and Correct Errors with XLM-Roberta

This alternative approach models the task as a two-stage prediction. The first stage involves detecting errors in the source data as a token labeling task. The second stage revolves around using a masked language model to generate a token as a replacement of a token labeled as an error in the first stage. In both stages, we used XLM-RoBERTa encoder-based language model (Conneau et al., 2020).

For the first stage, we need to create a labeled corpus from the source and gold essays. We apply a variant of the Needleman-Wunsch algorithm used to compute Levenshtein distance. In the classic algorithm, every error is given a weight of 1, which could cause some misalignment when there is a string of errors. To prevent misalignment of tokens, we give a (usually) lower weight to substitution edits to favor them instead of deletions and insertions. The actual weight for substitutions is computed using the `ratio` function provided by the python library called "Levenshtein"[3].

Once we have collected all the edit operations to transform an original sentence into its reference counterpart, we use these edits to create labels on the tokenized original sentence. Deletions (a token that is present in the original sentence but not the reference) are labeled "-". Insertions (a token from reference that should be added to the sentence) are ignored as they cannot be processed easily as part of a token classification task. Substitutions (when a token was in original sentence was partially aligned with a token in its reference counterpart) can be mapped to labels with a varying degree of granularity. We tried two variants: a coarse-grain and a fine-grain label scheme. In the fine-grain label scheme, we computed labels given predefined error types. We handled three casing modifications: to lower case, to upper case and to title case. We also modeled suffix modification for only the last letter, the tag is the letter to use to correct the token. Errors that did not fit into any previous case were given a generic error label marked as "<mask>". In the coarse-grain label scheme, only the "<mask>" label is used.

The token classification model is trained by fine-tuning XLM-RoBERTa embeddings with the flair library (Akbik et al., 2019).

For prediction, unlabeled essays are first tokenized using the syntok library[4]. The fine-tuned token classification model is then applied to label the data using the flair library. When the label represents a predefined correction to apply (to lower/upper case, substitute last letter, etc.), it is directly applied to the token. When a token is labeled with the generic error label, we apply XML-Roberta as a masked language model (MLM) to output the best token given the context of the sentence. The only optimization we tried is providing a threshold for the probability of the token that the MLM predicts. We used a threshold probability of 0.75 to apply a change. That is, the probability of

[3]The library is available at the following URL: `https://github.com/rapidfuzz/Levenshtein`

[4]https://github.com/fnl/syntok/

the predicted token by XLM-roberta has to be at least 0.75 or else the token is left unchanged.

In the end, labels other than "<mask>" and deletions were scarce and not well recognized by trained models. The final flair model used the coarse-grain label scheme.

4 Results

Systems are evaluated on automatic metrics categorized into two groups : reference-based metrics, including GLEU, Precision, Recall and $F_{0.5}$ scores, and reference-free metrics, represented by the Scribendi score. Precision, Recall, and $F_{0.5}$ scores are computed using a modified version of the ERRANT scorer (Bryant et al., 2017), with the $F_{0.5}$ score assigning twice the weight to precision compared to recall. Additionally, a human evaluation experiment is planned for a subset of submitted results following the shared task. The official evaluation was carried out on the CodaLab competition platform[5] based on the GLEU score.

In Table 4, we reported the official GLEU and F0.5 scores of our system and those of the baseline approach. Scores outperforming the baseline are reported in green; scores lower than the baseline in red. We note that we outperform the baseline for most languages, but we obtained very poor results for German, Icelandic and Slovene.

The failure with German is easy to explain: during the prediction phase, the system's execution was interrupted, not predicting all the needed output. , preventing it from predicting all the necessary output. Unfortunately, this issue was not noticed by our team, and we submitted an incomplete file. For the publication of this paper, we reran our pipeline correctly and obtained a GLEU score of 75.49 for this language.

However, for Icelandic and Slovene, we encountered serious problems. At first glance, the output appeared deviant, with the same sentences being repeated over and over. Therefore, we decided to submit the Icelandic corpus as it was, without modification, and to use the XLM-RoBERTa-based system for the Slovene dataset.

5 Discussion

5.1 Heterogeneity of the MultiGEC datasets

It is worth noting that the corpora exhibit high variability in annotation, which is crucial to consider when utilizing the MultiGEC dataset. The variation across corpora helps explain why developing one model per corpus yields better results than using one model per language.

For example, the choice of whether or not to capitalize addresses can differ from one corpus to another. Additionally, the learners of the language who wrote the original essays may come from different backgrounds. For instance, among the four different corpora for Czech, there are essays written by native students from elementary and secondary schools (NatForm), informal website texts (NatWebInf), essays written by Romani ethnic minority children and teenagers (Romani), and essays written by non-native speakers (Romani). The errors produced by these different profiles of speakers are undoubtedly specific to their age and social context, and therefore, the corrections are as well.

5.2 LLaMA-3.0's Pathological Output for Icelandic and Slovene

Our hypothesis is that these languages are ill supported by the LLaMA 3.0 model. Although Meta claims that it has been pre-trained on over 30 languages with high-quality data, non-English data accounts for only about 5% of the total pretraining corpus.[6]

We noticed that there is some Slovene Wikipedia data in LLaMA 3.0 (Touvron et al., 2023), but we suspect that it may not be sufficient. Additionally, the MultiGEC training data for Slovene are very limited. We found no evidence that LLaMA 3.0 possesses knowledge of Icelandic. This is further supported by an analysis of the tokenization performed by LLaMA.

If we look at the average number of characters per token for each set of essays, English, which is the default language of LLaMA, has 3.90 characters/token, German has 3.04 characters/token, Italian has 2.77 characters/token, and Icelandic has 1.83 and 1.87 characters/token (IceEC and IceL2EC, respectively), which is the lowest of all the languages present in the shared task data.

The average word length is 4.48 characters in English, and 4.31 and 4.65 characters (IceEC and IceL2EC, respectively) in Icelandic. Therefore, the token length difference cannot be explained by a word length difference alone. We suspect that this may be part of the explanation for the patho-

[5]https://codalab.lisn.upsaclay.fr/competitions/20500

[6]https://ai.meta.com/blog/meta-llama-3/

Language	Source	GLEU Lattice	GLEU Baseline	F0.5 Lattice	F0.5 Baseline
Czech	NatWebInf	**65.06**	53.91	**56.24**	32.93
	Romani	**53.70**	48.35	**45.99**	37.65
	SecLearn	**49.95**	45.77	**48.61**	46.18
	NatForm	71.45	76.08	31.99	37.46
English	Write & Improve	**77.90**	75.15	**53.79**	41.58
Estonian	EIC	**44.02**	36.47	22.73	24.38
	EKIL2	**56.96**	51.12	**38.07**	31.13
German	Merlin	0.05	69.56	14.09	52.58
Greek	GLCIIC	**51.49**	45.07	**44.07**	43.07
Icelandic	IceEC	**83.92**	80.52	0.00	8.19
	IceL2EC	39.79	39.93	0.00	8.14
Italian	Merlin	**69.96**	65.13	40.59	42.64
Latvian	LaVA	**67.25**	48.86	**57.77**	44.69
Russian	RULEC-GEC	77.77	79.02	**38.16**	34.71
Slovene	Solar-Eval	54.34	58.96	5.52	29.45
Swedish	SweLL_gold	**59.88**	58.40	40.01	41.46
Ukrainian	UA-GEC	**74.00**	68.03	**51.29**	22.66

Table 4: Comparison of our results with the baseline model on the minimal edits task. Results outperforming the baseline are highlighted in bold green, while those underperforming the baseline are in red.

logical behavior of our models with respect to this language.

Another reason for the poor performances of LLaMA seems to be the length of the essays. For all corpora except the Icelandic and Slovene ones, the average essay length is below 500 tokens (calculated with LLaMA's tokenizer), ranging from 33.6 tokens per essay on average for the Czech NatWebInf corpus to 460.8 tokens per essay for the Ukrainian UA_GEC corpus. English Write-AndImprove2024 essays is 188.8 tokens long on average. Slovene Solar-Eval essays are on average 1248.0 tokens long, the Icelandic IceL2EC essays are 1849.2 tokens long and the Icelandic IceEC essays are 2496.8 tokens long on average (calculated by the LLaMA tokenizer). Here again, the difference between Icelandic and English cannot simply be explained by the average token length difference. Icelandic essays are really longer than English ones and it seems that LLaMA has a harder time with longer inputs.

6 Distribution of Code

The code is available on GitHub under the MIT licence at the following address: https://github.com/lattice-8094/MultiGEC. It can be used to reproduce our results. Given the sensitivity of the data and the possibility of models leaking training data or hackers recovering the training data by inference attacks (Truex et al., 2021; Zhang et al., 2024), we will only distribute the program code. The data must be acquired by contacting the MultiGEC-2025 organizers. Researchers can obtain our models after making a personal request via email.

7 Conclusion and Future Work

We found that fine-tuning a multilingual large language model was a successful approach for most languages in the MultiGEC dataset, outperforming the baseline (using an LLM in a zero-shot setting). However, the model to be fine-tuned should have a minimal amount of knowledge about each target language for success. In this regard, we encountered difficulties with Slovenian and Icelandic.

Recently, we came across the Goldfish models (Chang et al., 2024): monolingual language models for 350 languages, including Icelandic and Slovenian, which propose smaller language models but with higher-quality data. It would be interesting to repeat the experiment using the Goldfish models and investigate whether the results for under-resourced languages can be improved.

References

Alan Akbik, Tanja Bergmann, Duncan Blythe, Kashif Rasul, Stefan Schweter, and Roland Vollgraf. 2019. FLAIR: An easy-to-use framework for state-of-the-art NLP. In *NAACL 2019, 2019 Annual Conference of the North American Chapter of the Association for Computational Linguistics (Demonstrations)*, pages 54–59.

Dan Biderman, Jacob Portes, Jose Javier Gonzalez Ortiz, Mansheej Paul, Philip Greengard, Connor Jennings, Daniel King, Sam Havens, Vitaliy Chiley, Jonathan Frankle, Cody Blakeney, and John P. Cunningham. 2024. Lora learns less and forgets less.

Christopher Bryant, Mariano Felice, and Ted Briscoe. 2017. Automatic annotation and evaluation of error types for grammatical error correction. In *Proceedings of the 55th Annual Meeting of the Association for Computational Linguistics (Volume 1: Long Papers)*, pages 793–805, Vancouver, Canada. Association for Computational Linguistics.

Christopher Bryant, Zheng Yuan, Muhammad Reza Qorib, Hannan Cao, Hwee Tou Ng, and Ted Briscoe. 2023. Grammatical error correction: A survey of the state of the art. *Computational Linguistics*, page 1–59.

Tyler A Chang, Catherine Arnett, Zhuowen Tu, and Benjamin K Bergen. 2024. Goldfish: Monolingual language models for 350 languages. *arXiv preprint arXiv:2408.10441*.

Alexis Conneau, Kartikay Khandelwal, Naman Goyal, Vishrav Chaudhary, Guillaume Wenzek, Francisco Guzmán, Edouard Grave, Myle Ott, Luke Zettlemoyer, and Veselin Stoyanov. 2020. Unsupervised cross-lingual representation learning at scale.

Christopher Davis, Andrew Caines, Oistein Andersen, Shiva Taslimipoor, Helen Yannakoudakis, Zheng Yuan, Christopher Bryant, Marek Rei, and Paula Buttery. 2024. Prompting open-source and commercial language models for grammatical error correction of english learner text. *ArXiv*, abs/2401.07702.

Tim Dettmers, Artidoro Pagnoni, Ari Holtzman, and Luke Zettlemoyer. 2024. Qlora: Efficient finetuning of quantized llms. *Advances in Neural Information Processing Systems*, 36.

Mengsay Loem, Masahiro Kaneko, Sho Takase, and Naoaki Okazaki. 2023. Exploring effectiveness of GPT-3 in grammatical error correction: A study on performance and controllability in prompt-based methods. In *Proceedings of the 18th Workshop on Innovative Use of NLP for Building Educational Applications (BEA 2023)*, pages 205–219, Toronto, Canada. Association for Computational Linguistics.

Arianna Masciolini, Andrew Caines, Orphée De Clercq, Joni Kruijsbergen, Murathan Kurfalı, Ricardo Muñoz Sánchez, Elena Volodina, and Robert Östling. 2025. The MultiGEC-2025 shared task on multilingual grammatical error correction at NLP4CALL. In *Proceedings of the 14th Workshop on Natural Language Processing for Computer Assisted Language Learning*, Tallin, Estonia. University of Tartu.

Grigori Sidorov, Anubhav Gupta, Martin Tozer, Dolors Catala, Angels Catena, and Sandrine Fuentes. 2013. Rule-based system for automatic grammar correction using syntactic n-grams for English language learning (L2). In *Proceedings of the Seventeenth Conference on Computational Natural Language Learning: Shared Task*, pages 96–101, Sofia, Bulgaria. Association for Computational Linguistics.

Hugo Touvron, Thibaut Lavril, Gautier Izacard, Xavier Martinet, Marie-Anne Lachaux, Timothée Lacroix, Baptiste Rozière, Naman Goyal, Eric Hambro, Faisal Azhar, et al. 2023. Llama: Open and efficient foundation language models. *arXiv preprint arXiv:2302.13971*.

Stacey Truex, Ling Liu, Mehmet Emre Gursoy, Lei Yu, and Wenqi Wei. 2021. Demystifying membership inference attacks in machine learning as a service. *IEEE Transactions on Services Computing*, 14(06):2073–2089.

Elena Volodina, Christopher Bryant, Andrew Caines, Orphée De Clercq, Jennifer-Carmen Frey, Elizaveta Ershova, Alexandr Rosen, and Olga Vinogradova. 2023. MultiGED-2023 shared task at NLP4CALL: Multilingual grammatical error detection. In *Proceedings of the 12th Workshop on NLP for Computer Assisted Language Learning*, pages 1–16, Tórshavn, Faroe Islands. LiU Electronic Press.

Zheng Yuan and Mariano Felice. 2013. Constrained grammatical error correction using statistical machine translation. In *Proceedings of the Seventeenth Conference on Computational Natural Language Learning: Shared Task*, pages 52–61, Sofia, Bulgaria. Association for Computational Linguistics.

Xinhao Zhang, Olga Seminck, and Pascal Amsili. 2024. Remember to forget: A study on verbatim memorization of literature in large language models. In *Proceedings of the Fifth Conference on Computational Humanities Research*, Aarhus, Danmark.

UAM-CSI at MultiGEC-2025: Parameter-efficient LLM Fine-tuning for Multilingual Grammatical Error Correction

Ryszard Staruch
Adam Mickiewicz University in Poznan
Center for Artificial Intelligence AMU
ryszard.staruch@amu.edu.pl

Abstract

This paper describes the solution of the UAM-CSI team to the shared task on Multilingual Grammatical Error Correction (MultiGEC-2025), which is part of the workshop on Natural Language Processing for Computer-Assisted Language Learning (NLP4CALL). The shared task covers 12 languages: Czech, English, Estonian, German, Greek, Icelandic, Italian, Latvian, Russian, Slovene, Swedish and Ukrainian. The aim of the task is to correct errors in the provided texts. Our system is a google/gemma-2-9b-it model with 2 QLoRA adapters, one for the minimal-edit track and another for the fluency-edit track. Our solution achieves the best performance on the test sets on GLEU and $F_{0.5}$ metrics for all languages and the best performance on the Scribendi Score metric except for the Greek language in the minimal-edit track.

1 Introduction

Grammatical Error Correction (GEC) is an NLP task that covers the detection and correction of all errors occurring in the given text. There are two main directions in the GEC field: the minimal-edit error correction and the fluency-edit error correction.

The first direction for English language is mostly concerned around second language learners in their learning process, which was carried out in published datasets, for example FCE (Yannakoudakis et al., 2011) and previous shared tasks: CoNLL-2014 (Ng et al., 2014) and BEA-2019 (Bryant et al., 2019). The most common measure of the effectiveness of the minimal-edit error correction systems is the $F_{0.5}$ score, which puts the higher weight for precision than recall.

The second direction for the English language focuses not only on correcting errors in texts but also on improving the fluency of the texts (Sakaguchi et al., 2016). There is only one dataset for English that was designed for the fluency-edit approach, the JFLEG dataset (Napoles et al., 2017). The primary metric for the JFLEG dataset is GLEU (Napoles et al., 2015), which is a modified version of BLEU (Papineni et al., 2002) that better fits the text correction task.

One of the main problems in GEC research is that most of the work is done only for the English language. There is ongoing research for other languages, mostly Chinese and Arabic, but there is an urgent need to address the lack of research on lesser-used languages. The biggest problem is mostly related to limited high-quality datasets, which are needed to create and evaluate GEC systems.

MultiGEC-2025 (Masciolini et al., 2025a) is the first shared task that covers many languages. It comes with the training, development and test datasets for each language. The task has two tracks: the minimal-edit track and the fluency-edit track. The novel feature of this shared task is that the texts are not divided on the sentence level, which was common practice in previous datasets. Systems are evaluated using three evaluation metrics: $F_{0.5}$, GLEU and Scribendi Score (Islam and Magnani, 2021). The Scribendi Score is a reference-free metric that uses a language model perplexity score to evaluate predictions. Using three metrics provides different perspectives on the quality of the submitted systems. It also enables the opportunity to analyze how different metrics behave across all datasets for solutions in the shared task, which will contribute to the research on the GEC evaluation.

In this paper, we describe two systems for the shared task, each for a different track. The organizers encouraged developing systems that are

Lang	Subcorpus	Learners	# Train	# Dev	# Test	# Total	# References
cs	NatWebInf	L1	3620	1291	1256	6167	2
cs	Romani	L1	3247	179	173	3599	2
cs	SecLearn	L2	2057	173	177	2407	2
cs	NatForm	L1	227	88	76	391	2
en	Write & Improve	L2	4040	506	504	5050	1
et	EIC	L2	206	26	26	258	3
et	EKIL2	L2	1202	150	151	1503	2
de	Merlin	L2	827	103	103	1033	1
el	GLCII	L2	1031	129	129	1289	1
is	IceEC	L1	140	18	18	176	1
is	IceL2EC	L2	155	19	19	193	1
it	Merlin	L2	651	81	81	813	1
lv	LaVA	L2	813	101	101	1015	1
ru	RULEC-GEC	mixed	2539	1969	1535	6043	3
sl	Solar-Eval	L1	10	50	49	109	1
sv	SweLL_gold	L2	402	50	50	502	1
uk	UA-GEC	mixed	1706	87	79	1872	4

Table 1: Overview of the subcorpora of the MultiGEC-2025 shared task with their sizes measured by the number of essays.

able to process all languages using a single model, which was done in our systems. We use the same architecture for both tracks: google/gemma-2-9b-it model (later denoted as Gemma 2) with QLoRA adapters, one for each track. The difference between systems is that the minimal-edit track system was fine-tuned only on one reference text for each dataset, whereas for the fluency-edit track, the system was fine-tuned on all reference texts. Our intuition behind this approach is that the model should produce more fluent output if it sees many ways to correct given text.

2 Related work

In recent years, there were a few research studies that covered Grammatical Error Correction for many languages. Rothe et al. (2021) describes two things that are needed to produce state-of-the-art multilingual GEC models. The first one focuses on generating synthetic datasets. The other one is to use multilingual language models that already possess the ability to use different languages. The important takeaway from this work is that larger models are needed to perform effectively on many languages.

One of the most recent works (Luhtaru et al., 2024) shows that leveraging decoder-only large language models (LLMs) as both synthetic data generators and correctors leads to state-of-the-art results for German, Estonian and Ukrainian languages.

Coyne et al. (2023) shows that instruction-tuned LLMs without task-specific fine-tuning are able to correct text better than fine-tuned models for the task when evaluating on the fluency-edit GEC dataset. If we think of the grammatical error correction as the task of making the text more probable, it could mean that the GEC task is directly related to the language modeling task. In the minimal-edit task we want to make more probable text in the parts that are clearly considered as erroneous, when for the fluency-edit task we can think more widely of making the text more probable. Then, the fine-tuning process should be mostly responsible for adjusting the way of correcting a given text, which is always subjective to the annotator.

These studies show that in order to create a promising single-model system capable of correcting text in many languages, it is necessary to use a pre-trained, large, multilingual language model that is fine-tuned to learn how to effectively correct errors in different languages.

3 Dataset overview

The dataset used in the MultiGEC-2025 shared task is a multilingual Grammatical Error Correction corpus (Masciolini et al., 2025b). It covers

Hyperparameter name	Value
learning rate	5e-5
batch size	4
gradient accumulation steps	4
warmup steps	40
lr scheduler	linear
epochs	2
optimizer	AdamW8bit
weight decay	0.01
threshold (max tokens)	300
LoRA rank	128
LoRA alpha	64

Table 2: Hyperparameter values used during fine-tuning.

12 European languages: Czech, English, Estonian, German, Greek, Icelandic, Italian, Latvian, Russian, Slovene, Swedish and Ukrainian. The dataset is divided into 17 subcorpora. The detailed statistics about the dataset can be found in Table 1.

It is worth noting that the size of the subcorpora is measured by the number of essays, whereas most existing datasets are divided and measured at the sentence level. It enables to take into consideration context of the whole text, which should be beneficial during the correction process. Czech, Estonian, Russian and Ukrainian datasets contain more than one correct reference. The texts in almost every dataset are written by either L1 or L2 learners. Only the RULEC-GEC and the UA-GEC corpora contain mixed types of text authors. This makes the task even more challenging because different types of learners make different errors.

4 System description

Due to the need to use a multilingual LLM and limited resources (a single Nvidia RTX 4090 card), we decided to go for the Gemma 2 model as it is one of the best performing multilingual models in its size. Its effectiveness could be related to the large vocabulary of 256k tokens and the fine-tuning process, which involves learning the entire probability distribution from the larger model rather than just predicting the next token in the sentence (Gemma Team et al., 2024). To be able to use a relatively large context, for which more VRAM is needed, we decided to use the 4-bit model quantization, 2 QLoRA adapters (Dettmers et al., 2024), one for each track, and the Unsloth framework (Daniel Han, 2023).

Some essays in the MultiGEC-2025 dataset are too long to load them into the model, thus the proper essay splitting algorithm is needed to fulfill two conditions:

1. Do not extend the maximum input length threshold (later denoted as **threshold**).

2. Use more than a single sentence as the input for the model, to make sure that the larger context than a single sentence is being used.

Our essay splitting algorithm is defined as follows:

1. If the number of essay tokens in both the source and target texts is below the threshold, add the text pair to the dataset. Otherwise, go to point 2.

2. Split the essay by newlines to get **paragraphs**. For each paragraph, if the number of essay tokens in both source and target texts is below the threshold append it to the dataset. Otherwise, go to point 3.

3. Split the paragraph on the sentence level using SaT model (Frohmann et al., 2024) to get **sentences**. Then, sentences are sequentially joined together until the source text or the target text created from sentences exceeds the threshold. After exceeding the threshold, the text pair is added to the dataset and the process is repeated for the remaining sentences.

The above algorithm for the development and test datasets are applied only for the source text part. The information for the paragraphs and sentences splits is saved to properly align the predictions from the model.

Both QLoRA adapters were fine-tuned using the same hyperparameters, described in Table 2. The adapters were fine-tuned only for 2 epochs, because fine-tuning for more epochs did not improve the results on all development subcorpora. Fine-tuning for a single epoch takes about 3 hours.

As mentioned in the Introduction, the only difference between adapters is that the adapter for the minimal-edit track was fine-tuned on the single, first reference from the dataset. The fluency-edit track QLoRA adapter was fine-tuned on all references. During fine-tuning, the datasets were combined and shuffled, so the adapters were fine-tuned on all languages at once.

Lang	Subcorpus	Track	P	R	$F_{0.5}$	GLEU	Scribendi
cs	NatWebInf	Minimal	69.81	63.95	68.55	69.89	0.79
		Fluency	71.05	64.28	69.58	70.04	0.79
cs	Romani	Minimal	59.94	50.13	57.68	60.07	0.92
		Fluency	59.23	50.18	57.17	60.23	0.91
cs	SecLearn	Minimal	62.58	47.23	58.76	55.81	0.98
		Fluency	62.21	46.50	58.27	55.16	0.99
cs	NatForm	Minimal	68.32	46.94	62.62	81.44	0.99
		Fluency	68.71	46.82	62.83	81.07	0.95
en	Write & Improve	Minimal	62.24	50.78	59.55	81.5	0.98
		Fluency	62.57	48.67	59.19	80.67	0.98
et	EIC	Minimal	54.39	36.23	49.44	55.76	1.0
		Fluency	56.79	38.6	51.9	57.89	1.0
et	EKIL2	Minimal	58.82	41.28	54.21	66.85	1.0
		Fluency	56.66	42.86	53.23	68.23	1.0
de	Merlin	Minimal	68.17	66.43	67.81	81.13	1.0
		Fluency	67.42	66.28	67.19	81.23	0.96
el	GLCII	Minimal	53.79	45.11	51.8	56.84	0.88
		Fluency	53.62	44.12	51.4	55.96	0.9
is	IceEC	Minimal	57.28	8.45	26.58	84.98	1.0
		Fluency	61.76	9.03	28.48	85.09	0.72
is	IceL2EC	Minimal	38.68	4.62	15.62	43.6	0.63
		Fluency	41.18	4.13	14.73	43.62	0.74
it	Merlin	Minimal	69.04	59.54	66.91	81.89	0.98
		Fluency	67.45	56.67	64.98	79.97	1.0
lv	LaVA	Minimal	80.77	78.32	80.27	84.5	1.0
		Fluency	79.76	78.54	79.51	84.65	1.0
ru	RULEC-GEC	Minimal	61.09	33.01	52.21	83.11	0.46
		Fluency	62.3	30.94	51.8	82.65	0.43
sl	Solar-Eval	Minimal	53.89	30.4	46.68	66.46	1.0
		Fluency	54.14	29.77	46.52	66.32	1.0
sv	SweLL_gold	Minimal	54.54	45.88	52.56	69.29	1.0
		Fluency	55.29	46.69	53.32	69.62	1.0
uk	UA-GEC	Minimal	74.31	54.11	69.15	79.55	0.89
		Fluency	74.65	55.02	69.68	79.82	0.8

Table 3: Results for the test sets for all MultiGEC-2025 shared task subcorpora.

5 Results

Table 3 shows our results for the test datasets for the minimal-edit track and the fluency-edit track. The systems for both tracks perform similarly across the datasets, although there are a few subcorpora with notable differences between the metric values.

For the $F_{0.5}$ score metric there are two subcorpora for which the differences are much larger compared to other datasets: the et/EIC dataset for the fluency-edit model and the it/Merlin dataset for the minimal-edit model. The et/EIC is one of the smallest datasets, so providing additional pairs for this subcorpus could be the reason for the improved results. On the other hand, for the it/Merlin dataset, adding more references for other languages might have caused worse results for other datasets, because adjusting model weights for one language could affect performance for the other languages. Although for most of the datasets the difference is much smaller.

The differences for the GLEU metric are similar to the $F_{0.5}$ score metric, which is expected since both metrics are reference-based metrics. Although, when looking at the results of the other participants[1] the results with low $F_{0.5}$ score metric have a relatively high GLEU metric value, because the unchanged text does not have a 0 value for the GLEU metric. This makes it more difficult to interpret the metric value compared to the $F_{0.5}$ score metric.

The results for the Scribendi Score metric are very high or perfect for almost all datasets, even if the $F_{0.5}$ score values are around 50%. The metric gives a discrete score of -1, 0, or 1 for each text, so minimal improvements in the text lead to the positive score, even if many errors in the text are not corrected. The metric should work better in the sentence-level GEC, because instead of a single score for the long text, there would be many scores for each sentence that could be averaged. It reveals the drawbacks of the metric and shows that there is a need for research in the reference-less GEC evaluation, especially for long texts.

6 Conclusions

This work shows that a single LLM can effectively correct text in many languages. Despite limited resources, our systems were able to achieve the highest scores for each track and for each metric across all datasets except for the Scribendi Score for the fluency-edit track for the GLCII dataset. Our essay splitting algorithm provides an efficient way to make use of longer parts of texts. The use of three metrics for the task revealed that $F_{0.5}$ still remains a useful and practical metric and that the Scribendi Score metric could be modified to better fit the long-text GEC.

The MultiGEC-2025 Shared Task makes a valuable contribution to multilingual grammatical error correction research and opens new paths for GEC researchers.

7 Limitations

Our system requires a modern graphics card to effectively run the model inference, which could be a problem for users who want to run the model on their devices. We only tested the models performance on the datasets provided in the shared task, so we do not know how effectively it corrects errors in other languages. We also did not test other language models due to the shared task deadlines. Our work does not include human evaluation or analysis of different types of errors, which could provide more insight into the performance of the system.

References

Christopher Bryant, Mariano Felice, Øistein E. Andersen, and Ted Briscoe. 2019. The BEA-2019 shared task on grammatical error correction. In *Proceedings of the Fourteenth Workshop on Innovative Use of NLP for Building Educational Applications*, pages 52–75, Florence, Italy. Association for Computational Linguistics.

Steven Coyne, Keisuke Sakaguchi, Diana Galvan-Sosa, Michael Zock, and Kentaro Inui. 2023. Analyzing the performance of gpt-3.5 and gpt-4 in grammatical error correction.

Unsloth team Daniel Han, Michael Han. 2023. Unsloth.

Tim Dettmers, Artidoro Pagnoni, Ari Holtzman, and Luke Zettlemoyer. 2024. Qlora: efficient finetuning of quantized llms. In *Proceedings of the 37th International Conference on Neural Information Processing Systems*, NIPS '23, Red Hook, NY, USA. Curran Associates Inc.

Markus Frohmann, Igor Sterner, Ivan Vulić, Benjamin Minixhofer, and Markus Schedl. 2024. Segment any text: A universal approach for robust, efficient and adaptable sentence segmentation. In *Proceedings of*

[1]`https://spraakbanken.github.io/multigec-2025/shared_task.html#results`

the 2024 Conference on Empirical Methods in Natural Language Processing, pages 11908–11941, Miami, Florida, USA. Association for Computational Linguistics.

Gemma Team, Morgane Riviere, Shreya Pathak, Pier Giuseppe Sessa, Cassidy Hardin, Surya Bhupatiraju, Léonard Hussenot, Thomas Mesnard, Bobak Shahriari, Alexandre Ramé, Johan Ferret, Peter Liu, Pouya Tafti, Abe Friesen, Michelle Casbon, Sabela Ramos, Ravin Kumar, Charline Le Lan, Sammy Jerome, Anton Tsitsulin, Nino Vieillard, Piotr Stanczyk, Sertan Girgin, Nikola Momchev, Matt Hoffman, Shantanu Thakoor, Jean-Bastien Grill, Behnam Neyshabur, Olivier Bachem, Alanna Walton, Aliaksei Severyn, Alicia Parrish, Aliya Ahmad, Allen Hutchison, Alvin Abdagic, Amanda Carl, Amy Shen, Andy Brock, Andy Coenen, Anthony Laforge, Antonia Paterson, Ben Bastian, Bilal Piot, Bo Wu, Brandon Royal, Charlie Chen, Chintu Kumar, Chris Perry, Chris Welty, Christopher A. Choquette-Choo, Danila Sinopalnikov, David Weinberger, Dimple Vijaykumar, Dominika Rogozińska, Dustin Herbison, Elisa Bandy, Emma Wang, Eric Noland, Erica Moreira, Evan Senter, Evgenii Eltyshev, Francesco Visin, Gabriel Rasskin, Gary Wei, Glenn Cameron, Gus Martins, Hadi Hashemi, Hanna Klimczak-Plucińska, Harleen Batra, Harsh Dhand, Ivan Nardini, Jacinda Mein, Jack Zhou, James Svensson, Jeff Stanway, Jetha Chan, Jin Peng Zhou, Joana Carrasqueira, Joana Iljazi, Jocelyn Becker, Joe Fernandez, Joost van Amersfoort, Josh Gordon, Josh Lipschultz, Josh Newlan, Ju yeong Ji, Kareem Mohamed, Kartikeya Badola, Kat Black, Katie Millican, Keelin McDonell, Kelvin Nguyen, Kiranbir Sodhia, Kish Greene, Lars Lowe Sjoesund, Lauren Usui, Laurent Sifre, Lena Heuermann, Leticia Lago, Lilly McNealus, Livio Baldini Soares, Logan Kilpatrick, Lucas Dixon, Luciano Martins, Machel Reid, Manvinder Singh, Mark Iverson, Martin Görner, Mat Velloso, Mateo Wirth, Matt Davidow, Matt Miller, Matthew Rahtz, Matthew Watson, Meg Risdal, Mehran Kazemi, Michael Moynihan, Ming Zhang, Minsuk Kahng, Minwoo Park, Mofi Rahman, Mohit Khatwani, Natalie Dao, Nenshad Bardoliwalla, Nesh Devanathan, Neta Dumai, Nilay Chauhan, Oscar Wahltinez, Pankil Botarda, Parker Barnes, Paul Barham, Paul Michel, Pengchong Jin, Petko Georgiev, Phil Culliton, Pradeep Kuppala, Ramona Comanescu, Ramona Merhej, Reena Jana, Reza Ardeshir Rokni, Rishabh Agarwal, Ryan Mullins, Samaneh Saadat, Sara Mc Carthy, Sarah Cogan, Sarah Perrin, Sébastien M. R. Arnold, Sebastian Krause, Shengyang Dai, Shruti Garg, Shruti Sheth, Sue Ronstrom, Susan Chan, Timothy Jordan, Ting Yu, Tom Eccles, Tom Hennigan, Tomas Kocisky, Tulsee Doshi, Vihan Jain, Vikas Yadav, Vilobh Meshram, Vishal Dharmadhikari, Warren Barkley, Wei Wei, Wenming Ye, Woohyun Han, Woosuk Kwon, Xiang Xu, Zhe Shen, Zhitao Gong, Zichuan Wei, Victor Cotruta, Phoebe Kirk, Anand Rao, Minh Giang, Ludovic Peran, Tris Warkentin, Eli Collins, Joelle Barral, Zoubin Ghahramani, Raia Hadsell, D. Sculley, Jeanine Banks, Anca Dragan, Slav Petrov, Oriol Vinyals, Jeff Dean, Demis Hassabis, Koray Kavukcuoglu, Clement Farabet, Elena Buchatskaya, Sebastian Borgeaud, Noah Fiedel, Armand Joulin, Kathleen Kenealy, Robert Dadashi, and Alek Andreev. 2024. Gemma 2: Improving open language models at a practical size.

Md Asadul Islam and Enrico Magnani. 2021. Is this the end of the gold standard? a straightforward reference-less grammatical error correction metric. In *Proceedings of the 2021 Conference on Empirical Methods in Natural Language Processing*, pages 3009–3015, Online and Punta Cana, Dominican Republic. Association for Computational Linguistics.

Agnes Luhtaru, Taido Purason, Martin Vainikko, Maksym Del, and Mark Fishel. 2024. To err is human, but llamas can learn it too. In *Findings of the Association for Computational Linguistics: EMNLP 2024*, pages 12466–12481, Miami, Florida, USA. Association for Computational Linguistics.

Arianna Masciolini, Andrew Caines, Orphée De Clercq, Joni Kruijsbergen, Murathan Kurfalı, Ricardo Muñoz Sánchez, Elena Volodina, and Robert Östling. 2025a. The MultiGEC-2025 shared task on multilingual grammatical error correction at NLP4CALL. In *Proceedings of the 14th Workshop on Natural Language Processing for Computer Assisted Language Learning*, Tallin, Estonia. University of Tartu.

Arianna Masciolini, Andrew Caines, Orphée De Clercq, Joni Kruijsbergen, Murathan Kurfalı, Ricardo Muñoz Sánchez, Elena Volodina, Robert Östling, Kais Allkivi, Špela Arhar Holdt, Ilze Auzina, Roberts Darģis, Elena Drakonaki, Jennifer-Carmen Frey, Isidora Glišić, Pinelopi Kikilintza, Lionel Nicolas, Mariana Romanyshyn, Alexandr Rosen, Alla Rozovskaya, Kristjan Suluste, Oleksiy Syvokon, Alexandros Tantos, Despoina-Ourania Touriki, Konstantinos Tsiotskas, Eleni Tsourilla, Vassilis Varsamopoulos, Katrin Wisniewski, Aleš Žagar, and Torsten Zesch. 2025b. Towards better language representation in Natural Language Processing – a multilingual dataset for text-level Grammatical Error Correction. *International Journal of Learner Corpus Research.*

Courtney Napoles, Keisuke Sakaguchi, Matt Post, and Joel Tetreault. 2015. Ground truth for grammatical error correction metrics. In *Proceedings of the 53rd Annual Meeting of the Association for Computational Linguistics and the 7th International Joint Conference on Natural Language Processing (Volume 2: Short Papers)*, pages 588–593, Beijing, China. Association for Computational Linguistics.

Courtney Napoles, Keisuke Sakaguchi, and Joel Tetreault. 2017. JFLEG: A fluency corpus and benchmark for grammatical error correction. In *Proceedings of the 15th Conference of the European Chapter of the Association for Computational Linguistics: Volume 2, Short Papers*, pages 229–234,

Valencia, Spain. Association for Computational Linguistics.

Hwee Tou Ng, Siew Mei Wu, Ted Briscoe, Christian Hadiwinoto, Raymond Hendy Susanto, and Christopher Bryant. 2014. The CoNLL-2014 shared task on grammatical error correction. In *Proceedings of the Eighteenth Conference on Computational Natural Language Learning: Shared Task*, pages 1–14, Baltimore, Maryland. Association for Computational Linguistics.

Kishore Papineni, Salim Roukos, Todd Ward, and Wei-Jing Zhu. 2002. Bleu: a method for automatic evaluation of machine translation. In *Proceedings of the 40th Annual Meeting of the Association for Computational Linguistics*, pages 311–318, Philadelphia, Pennsylvania, USA. Association for Computational Linguistics.

Sascha Rothe, Jonathan Mallinson, Eric Malmi, Sebastian Krause, and Aliaksei Severyn. 2021. A simple recipe for multilingual grammatical error correction. In *Proceedings of the 59th Annual Meeting of the Association for Computational Linguistics and the 11th International Joint Conference on Natural Language Processing (Volume 2: Short Papers)*, pages 702–707, Online. Association for Computational Linguistics.

Keisuke Sakaguchi, Courtney Napoles, Matt Post, and Joel Tetreault. 2016. Reassessing the goals of grammatical error correction: Fluency instead of grammaticality. *Transactions of the Association for Computational Linguistics*, 4:169–182.

Helen Yannakoudakis, Ted Briscoe, and Ben Medlock. 2011. A new dataset and method for automatically grading ESOL texts. In *Proceedings of the 49th Annual Meeting of the Association for Computational Linguistics: Human Language Technologies*, pages 180–189, Portland, Oregon, USA. Association for Computational Linguistics.

A Prompt used during fine-tuning

Both adapters were fine-tuned using the same prompt. The following prompt was used:

Correct the following text, making only minimal changes where necessary.

Text to correct:

(text to correct)

Corrected text:

(corrected text)

B Requirements needed to run the model

The model requires 8.8GB of VRAM to be loaded into the graphics card. Additional VRAM is also required for the inference, so a graphics card with 12 GB of VRAM is the minimum requirement that is needed to run the inference, although more VRAM allows the batch size to be increased and the cache to be used.

Interpretable Machine Learning for Societal Language Identification: Modeling English and German Influences on Portuguese Heritage Language

Soroosh Akef[1,2] **Detmar Meurers**[3,2] **Amália Mendes**[1] **Patrick Rebuschat**[4,2]
[1]Center of Linguistics of the University of Lisbon, Portugal
[2]LEAD Graduate School and Research Network, University of Tübingen, Germany
[3]Leibniz Institute für Wissensmedien (IWM), Germany
[4]Lancaster University, United Kingdom
sorooshakef@edu.ulisboa.pt d.meurers@iwm-tuebingen.de
mendes@edu.ulisboa.pt p.rebuschat@lancaster.ac.uk

Abstract

This study leverages interpretable machine learning to investigate how different societal languages (SLs) influence the written production of Portuguese heritage language (HL) learners. Using a corpus of learner texts from adolescents in Germany and the UK, we systematically control for topic and proficiency level to isolate the cross-linguistic effects that each SL may exert on the HL. We automatically extract a wide range of linguistic complexity measures, including lexical, morphological, syntactic, discursive, and grammatical measures, and apply clustering-based undersampling to ensure balanced and representative data. Utilizing an explainable boosting machine, a class of inherently interpretable machine learning models, our approach identifies predictive patterns that discriminate between English- and German-influenced HL texts. The findings highlight distinct lexical and morphosyntactic patterns associated with each SL, with some patterns in the HL mirroring the structures of the SL. These results support the role of the SL in characterizing HL output. Beyond offering empirical evidence of cross-linguistic influence, this work demonstrates how interpretable machine learning can serve as an empirical test bed for language acquisition research.

1 Introduction

Cross-linguistic influence (CLI), or language transfer, broadly refers to the ways in which the linguistic representations of multilingual speakers interact with and affect one another. In the past several decades, this phenomenon has been a central issue of second language acquisition (SLA) research, as how a learner's L1 can shape the trajectory of L2 development has been extensively investigated (Odlin, 2022). Although the initial focus of CLI research was on the L1 transfer effect on L2, it is now believed that linguistic representations within the mind of a multilingual resemble a web, with complex interactions between all their linguistic systems (Macwhinney, 1987; McManus, 2021). The insights gained from this line of research have not only contributed to our understanding of the processes involved in language acquisition, but have also had implications for instructed SLA (McManus, 2019). Nevertheless, the focus of CLI research thus far has disproportionately been on L2 and its interaction with L1, with far less attention being given to CLI in other bilingual settings, particularly that of heritage language (HL) learners.

HL learners are individuals who grow up in an environment where a minority language is spoken at home while a dominant societal language (SL) is spoken in the broader community, possibly as a result of immigration (Benmamoun et al., 2013). Such learners often acquire their HL in naturalistic family settings during childhood, even as their formal education and daily social interactions are primarily conducted in the SL. Over time, the HL may develop differently than it would in a majority-language environment, resulting in a divergent outcome from that of native speakers who acquired their language in their home country (Bayram et al., 2019). While this divergence has been attributed to many factors, including the lower quality and quantity of input (Flores and Barbosa, 2014), the influence of the SL has been

Soroosh Akef, Detmar Meurers, Amália Mendes and Patrick Rebuschat. Interpretable Machine Learning for Societal Language Identification: Modeling English and German Influences on Portuguese Heritage Language. *Proceedings of the 14th Workshop on Natural Language Processing for Computer Assisted Language Learning (NLP4CALL 2025).* University of Tartu Library. 50–62.

discussed as a contributor (Scontras et al., 2015) even though the empirical evidence for this influence has been mixed (van Osch, 2019; Torregrossa et al., 2023). This lack of conclusive evidence calls for more exploratory studies leveraging broad linguistic features that potentially capture the effect of the SL on HL production, particularly at various stages of development.

A critical gap involves understanding whether and how different SLs might variably influence the same HL. To date, comparisons that explicitly investigate how distinct SLs shape the development of a single HL have been limited, prompting Scontras et al. (2015) to call for such studies. Such comparisons could also contribute to our understanding of the impact of typological proximity, lexical overlap, and structural similarity on the development of the HL.

Consequently, our study aims to address this gap by examining the influence of two distinct, albeit typologically and genetically related, SLs (German and English) on the production of a single HL, European Portuguese. We employ a range of computational tools and methodologies, including the automatic extraction of linguistic complexity measures, topic modeling, clustering-based undersampling, and the application of interpretable machine learning models, to determine whether these models can reliably distinguish between HL texts produced in different SL contexts, a task we refer to as societal language identification (SLI). Specifically, we address the following research question: Can a machine learning model distinguish between texts produced by Portuguese HL learners with different SLs (English or German) using a wide range of linguistic complexity measures? By focusing on the types of linguistic complexity measures that distinguish between these two learner groups, we aim to identify patterns that may mirror tendencies of the respective SLs and in doing so, demonstrate the benefits of utilizing interpretable machine learning as an empirical test bed.

Beyond its theoretical implications, this task includes considerable practical significance: Insights gained from this line of research can inform the design of more personalized intelligent computer-assisted language learning (ICALL) systems that are geared to the unique needs of HL learners with different SL backgrounds. Drawing on the noticing hypothesis (Schmidt, 1990), which posits that mere exposure is insufficient for language acquisition and that learners must consciously pay attention to linguistic features of their input to acquire them, such systems can be designed to provide targeted exposure through input enhancement (Meurers et al., 2010) and input enrichment (Chinkina and Meurers, 2016), addressing specific areas of weakness. Taking different language backgrounds into account is also needed to draw valid inferences about learner competencies in Intelligent Tutoring Systems (Amaral and Meurers, 2008). Furthermore, understanding the specific ways in which SLs influence HL production is essential to ensure fairness in automatic language proficiency testing. Incorporating features that consistently predict proficiency across different SL or L1 backgrounds could mitigate potential biases that may unfairly disadvantage certain learner groups.

In the following sections, we begin with a review of the related work on CLI as it relates to HL acquisition and the task of native language identification (NLI), a task similar to, yet distinct from, the current task of SLI. Subsequently, we describe the methodology of our experiment, including the corpus of Portuguese HL texts, the automatic extraction of linguistic complexity measures, our attempt of controlling for text topic and balancing the data, and the interpretable machine learning approach utilized. This is followed by a presentation of the results, where we highlight the key findings related to the distinctions between English- and German-speaking HL learners. Finally, we discuss the theoretical and practical implications of these findings for the characterization of HLs, and we conclude with directions for future research.

2 Related Work

2.1 Cross-Linguistic Influence on the Heritage Language

CLI in bilingual development is a multifaceted phenomenon affecting HL acquisition across various linguistic domains. The lexicon is often considered to be a linguistic domain which is highly susceptible to CLI. In their investigation of English HL speakers with Hebrew as the SL, Gordon and Meir (2024) found no effect of CLI on morphosyntax, yet significant differences between the HL groups and the baseline group with regard to lexicon were observed. Specifically, heritage speakers exhibited minor lexical production errors influenced by Hebrew. Similarly, Böttcher and Zellers (2024) investigated how Russian HL speakers in contact with English or German increased their use of vocalic-nasal filler particles, a pattern reflecting the tendencies of the SL. Such effects are indicative of the subtle ways CLI can manifest itself in the HL.

On the other hand, while some research suggests that morphology and syntax are more resistant to CLI than the lexicon, other studies have found that the SL can influence HL morphosyntax: Meir and Janssen (2021) demonstrated how Russian HL speakers in contact with Dutch or Hebrew struggled to produce accusative and genitive morphology with the same accuracy as monolingual Russian speakers, concluding that differences in the mapping of functional features influence HL morphological acquisition. Cuza (2013) similarly demonstrated how the absence of subject-verb inversion in English influenced Spanish HL speakers, making them struggle with inversion in embedded questions. Likewise, Seo and Cuza (2024) found that Korean HL speakers in an English-dominant environment overused demonstratives and underused bare nouns, patterns mirroring English nominal structures. Furthermore, Brehmer and Usanova (2015) reported that Russian HL speakers in Germany exhibited increased verb-final structures, possibly as a result of German CLI, yet they preserved other HL-specific pragmatic patterns.

Meanwhile, Fridman et al. (2024) found CLI to be a main mechanism behind HL grammar maintenance in adults across multiple morphosyntactic phenomena (i.e., adjective–noun agreement, accusative case morphology, and numerical phrases) among Russian HL speakers in Hebrew and English environments. Notably, while CLI was found to be a major predictor of HL grammar maintenance, increased input and proficiency were found to modulate its effects. By contrast, other studies, such as Verkhovtceva et al. (2023), reported no clear evidence of CLI in HL morphosyntax, attributing the observed variation primarily to the age of onset of bilingualism. Similarly, Torregrossa et al. (2023) did not find CLI to significantly affect the performance of Portuguese HL children from three different SLs on a cloze-test targeting various linguistic structures, pointing to the variability in whether and how CLI manifests.

Despite the fact that many studies that attempt to isolate the role of CLI utilize monolingual speakers as the baseline group, Rothman et al. (2023) have criticized this approach due to its assumption that the HL is deficient and that its speakers must strive to conform to the monolingual norm. In lieu of this approach, one of the alternative approaches they have recommended is comparing bilingual groups from different SLs, which can allow us to capture possible differences in their language use as a result of CLI without the implication of HL deficiency.

2.2 Text-Based Native Language Identification

While the present study deals with identifying the SL in the context of HL development, text-based NLI is a closely related task, whose techniques can be transferred to SLI. NLI seeks to determine an author's L1 based on their productions in a specific L2. Although the goal in our task differs, both NLI and SLI involve identifying subtle linguistic fingerprints of previously acquired or concurrently acquiring languages on a target language.

NLI has become an established task in computational linguistics, as evidenced by several shared tasks in the last decade (Tetreault et al., 2013; Malmasi et al., 2017; M et al., 2018). Studies in NLI, surveyed comprehensively by Goswami et al. (2024), have explored a variety of feature sets and modeling approaches.

The features used for this task range from shallow features such as n-grams (Mohammadi et al., 2017) and part-of-speech (POS) information (Malmasi and Dras, 2018) to lexical features (Malmasi and Dras, 2014) and syntactic features (Bykh and Meurers, 2014). Nevertheless, Goswami et al. (2024) warn that despite the success of n-grams in NLI, their success may be attributed to capturing thematic differences likely to be present in texts produced by learners coming from different countries, as learners tend to make references to aspects of their home country in their texts, which an n-gram model can exploit. In essence, n-grams fail to utilize features that are informative about the language development of learners. This highlights the importance of using features which not only result in the best model performance, but which also validly characterize the construct being modeled, which can ultimately result in better model generalizability (Akef et al., 2024).

The models having been used for NLI resemble most other machine learning tasks, covering a range of traditional machine learning classifiers, such as SVMs (Bykh et al., 2013), logistic regression (Vajjala and Banerjee, 2017), and ensemble classifiers (Malmasi and Dras, 2018); deep learning approaches, such as gated recurrent unit (Bhargava et al., 2017), and long short-term memory (Mundotiya et al., 2018); as well as more recent approaches leveraging large language models (Zhang and Salle, 2023).

While the focus of the vast majority of NLI attempts has been on achieving superior accuracy, there exists tangible value in investing more effort in investigating whether the manner in which a given model makes its predictions aligns with theories conceptualizing the construct being modeled. Moreover, interpretable machine learning approaches, defined as algorithms that not only identify patterns in the data to perform a particular task but that can be studied to gain insights into and extract knowledge from the data (in contrast to end-to-end black-box models) (Murdoch et al., 2019), can serve as an empirical test bed to map the possible effects of a broad range of predictors in a way that is unfeasible using traditional statistical analysis techniques.

3 Methodology

3.1 Data

The data analyzed in this study originate from texts produced by HL learners as part of the annual EPE certificate examination[1], organized by the Camões Institute, which is administered to Portuguese HL learners residing abroad. The Camões Institute, an institution affiliated with the Portuguese Ministry of Foreign Affairs, is charged with promoting Portuguese language and culture worldwide. Through its educational programs, including community schools and language courses, the Institute supports Portuguese families abroad and ensures that their children maintain a connection to their linguistic heritage. This particular examination targets adolescents (aged 15–18) who have grown up in Germany or the UK and are receiving formal instruction in Portuguese as a HL.

Table 1 illustrates the distribution of the corpus across the two societal languages (German and English) and the three Common European Framework of Reference for Languages (CEFR) (Council of Europe, 2001) proficiency levels of B1, B2, and C1. The corpus, containing a total of 472 texts with an average word count of 162.03, has a relatively balanced distribution across the CEFR levels for the German group while there are relatively fewer texts in the B2 and C1 levels in the English group.

To ensure that differences attributed to the SL are not merely as a result of possible topic difference, it was necessary to control for text topic prior to training. To this end, topic modeling using latent Dirichlet allocation (LDA) (Blei et al., 2003) was performed on the entire corpus using the Gensim Python library (Řehůřek and Sojka, 2010). By iteratively calculating the semantic coherence score (Mimno et al., 2011) of up to ten topics, the following nine topics were identified in the corpus based on the most representative words for each topic:

1. Personal life and relationships
2. Technologies, libraries, and youth
3. Travel and accommodation
4. Art, tourism, and cultural activities
5. Future and virtual reality
6. Books, culture, and leisure
7. Nature and outdoor photography
8. Tablets, education, and everyday tech
9. Work and projects

Subsequently, topics 1, 3, 4, and 6 were deemed similar enough to be grouped under one general topic of *Personal, cultural, and recreational life* to minimize data loss while adequately controlling for text topic. Subsequent to this step, a total of 298 texts belonging to this general topic were kept in the dataset, whose distribution across CEFR levels and SL is displayed in Table 2

By focusing on a single, thematically homogeneous subset of texts, we ensure that differences in linguistic complexity and structure are not confounded by text topic.

[1]https://www.instituto-camoes.pt/en/index.php?Itemid=2924

	B1	B2	C1	Total
English	90 (53.3%)	37 (21.9%)	42 (24.8%)	169 (100%)
German	102 (33.7%)	100 (33.0%)	101 (33.3%)	303 (100%)

Table 1: Distribution of texts by SL and CEFR proficiency level.

	B1	B2	C1	Total
English	76 (59.8%)	34 (26.8%)	17 (13.4%)	127 (100%)
German	46 (26.9%)	58 (33.9%)	67 (39.2%)	171 (100%)

Table 2: Distribution of texts on the selected general topic by SL and CEFR proficiency level.

3.2 Features

A total of 653 linguistic complexity features were automatically extracted from the texts partly using CTAP (Chen and Meurers, 2016; Weiss and Meurers, 2019), a web-based linguistic complexity analyzer which has been expanded to support a number of languages, including Portuguese (Demattos, 2020; Ribeiro-Flucht et al., 2024), and partly using custom annotators we developed to identify European Portuguese constructions using the rule-based matching of the spaCy Python library (Honnibal et al., 2020). Linguistic complexity is often defined in terms of the degree of variety and sophistication of a language instance (Wolfe-Quintero, 1998) or in terms of how challenging a language instance is (Ellis and Barkhuizen, 2005). However, the features used in this study vary in terms of the theoretical perspectives to complexity, including structural complexity measures, operationalized in terms of the number and variety of linguistic properties (Bulté and Housen, 2012; Pallotti, 2015) to measures of developmental complexity, such as age of acquisition, and processing complexity, such as concreteness. Table 3 demonstrates the distribution of these features across various classes, and the full list of features is available on the study's OSF repository[2].

Count-based features indicate the raw counts of various linguistic units, such as tokens, clauses, or particular syntactic structures. While these features could be categorized under syntactic complexity since longer linguistic units often imply higher syntactic complexity, the length-dependent nature of them necessitates different treatment from normalized syntactic features. Count-based features include measures such as the number of agent modifiers or the number of complex noun phrases.

[2]https://osf.io/8gqud/

Lexical features form the largest category of features in this study. They capture the sophistication and richness of the vocabulary by examining, for instance, various forms of type-token ratio (root, logarithmic, corrected, standard), as well as frequency-based measures such as word frequency per million. In addition to these traditional lexical features, psycholinguistic measures, such as age of acquisition and imageability, which stem from psycholinguistic experiments on how words are processed, are also included in this feature class.

On the other hand, syntactic features quantify aspects such as the frequency and depth of subordinate clauses, the presence of particular phrase types, or the mean length of clauses. For example, features including prepositional phrase types per token or the rate of subordination shed light on the learners' ability to produce more complex syntactic constructions.

Morphological features gauge the complexity resulting from inflectional and derivational processes. They provide information about how effectively learners manipulate the morphological structures of Portuguese, including person, number, tense, and mood markers. Examples include measures such as first person per word token or indicatives per word token.

Another class of complexity features extracted are discursive features, which measure cohesion at the text level. This class uses the frequency and variety of discourse markers as a feature characterizing the cohesiveness of the language.

Finally, this study utilizes a set of grammatical complexity features based on the occurrence of various European Portuguese constructions. Guided by the *Referencial Camões*[3], a benchmark specifying at which levels of proficiency specific

[3]https://www.instituto-camoes.pt/activity/centro-virtual/referencial-camoes-ple

Class	Count-based	Lexical	Syntactic	Discursive	Morphological	Grammatical
Count	182	241	73	42	32	83

Table 3: Count of features by class.

European Portuguese structures should be taught, these features are designed to serve as criterial features (Hawkins and Buttery, 2010) whose consistent use can be indicative of a learner having reached a specific proficiency level. While there could be overlap between this class and other linguistic complexity classes, they are classified separately due to their expected capacity to distinguish between proficiency levels.

By utilizing these diverse feature sets ranging from shallow token counts and POS categories to sophisticated lexical, morphological, syntactic, and language-specific grammatical complexity measures, we create a rich representation for each text, well suited to detecting differences in language use that may arise from the influence of the SL. Moreover, it aligns with our goal of employing an interpretable machine learning model, as we can better understand the ways in which the SL affects the HL across various linguistic domains.

3.2.1 Justifying Broad Linguistic Complexity Modeling

Criticism has been leveled against experiments such as the current study, in which a broad set of linguistic complexity measures extracted based on different theoretical frameworks are utilized to study linguistic phenomena, with Bulté et al. (2024) likening this approach to p-hacking. However, this critique mischaracterizes the intent and methodology of our approach, which is fundamentally data-driven and aims to discover patterns rather than simply confirm pre-existing theoretical assumptions. While we acknowledge the importance of careful selection of predictors for hypothesis testing, our methodology contributes to a different stage of the cycle of scientific progress, namely data-driven discovery and theory-informed interpretation.

To extend the analogy used by Jarvis (2010), where asserting the existence of CLI effects are likened to establishing the guilt of a defendent in a criminal trial, our approach is analogous to a detective investigating a crime. Rather than start with a single theory about the perpetrator's motive, the detective gathers all available evidence that might possibly offer a clue, from DNA samples and fingerprints to witness testimonies and purchase records. This broad data collection allows for the discovery of unexpected connections and the subsequent development of a more comprehensive understanding of the crime. Similarly, we cast a wide net in terms of linguistic features, drawing inspiration from various theoretical perspectives on what might be relevant to SL influence. Hence, we do not presuppose the primacy of any single theoretical framework, but rather allow the data itself, through machine learning, to reveal which features are most informative. Our approach, therefore, can be characterized as exploratory data analysis (EDA) for hypothesis generation rather than confirmatory analysis through hypothesis testing (Carmichael and Marron, 2018), both of which are essential steps of scientific progress.

The key difference between our approach and p-hacking lies in the purpose of feature selection. While p-hacking involves iteratively testing numerous hypotheses and selectively reporting only those that achieve statistical significance, our goal is not to confirm pre-defined hypotheses about specific features, but rather to explore the feature space and identify which linguistic features are most capable of characterizing CLI. Subsequently, this data-driven feature selection informs theoretical interpretation and model building, which has shown to result in better model accuracy and generalizability (Bykh and Meurers, 2016; Bykh et al., 2013; Akef et al., 2024).

3.3 Clustering-Based Downsampling

To ensure that both SLs were equally represented at each proficiency level and to prevent model biases arising from imbalanced class distributions, a clustering-based downsampling technique was employed (Lin et al., 2017). The corpus on the selected topic initially contained a larger number of texts produced by German-speakers relative to English-speakers, particularly at the B2 and C1 levels. Without adjusting for these discrepancies, the resulting model could be influenced more strongly by the SL with greater representation, making it difficult to attribute observed linguistic patterns to the SL rather than sampling imbalance.

To this end, the dataset was divided into English and German subgroups for each CEFR proficiency level, with the goal of downsampling the larger subgroup to match the size of the smaller subgroup. To ensure that the selected samples from the majority subgroup remained representative of its overall distribution, a two-step dimensionality reduction and clustering process was employed. Specifically, the scikit-learn (Pedregosa et al., 2018) implementation of the principal component analysis (PCA) algorithm was utilized to reduce the dimensionality of the feature space from 653 features to 10 principal components. PCA serves to capture the most significant variance in the data while mitigating the noise and potential curse of dimensionality that could adversely affect the downstream clustering step.

Following dimensionality reduction, K-means clustering (also from scikit-learn) was applied to the lower-dimensional data. The number of clusters (K) for K-means was set to the size of the minority subgroup: 46, 34, and 17 for levels B1, B2, and C1 respectively. By calculating pairwise distances between the texts and the cluster centroids, the sample with the smallest distance to each centroid was selected as its representative.

Finally, these selected samples from the majority group were combined with all samples from the minority group to form a balanced subset at each proficiency level. By repeating this procedure for each level and concatenating the balanced subsets, a new dataset was obtained in which English and German texts are equally represented at each proficiency level, as demonstrated in Table 4.

While other methods such as upsampling could also address class imbalance, downsampling was chosen here to preserve the variance in the data. Upsampling through simple duplication or synthetic generation of minority-class texts could introduce biased patterns and potentially result in unrepresentative interpretation of the model's use of features to distinguish between the two SLs.

3.4 Training

To model the influence of the SL on the HL, this study employs explainable boosting machines (EBMs) (Nori et al., 2019), a class of inherently interpretable machine learning models. EBMs are a type of generalized additive model (GAM) that leverage gradient boosting while maintaining a transparent structure. Consequently, EBMs construct predictions as a sum of shape functions for each individual feature and specified feature interactions. This architecture makes it possible to reliably identify which features and interactions play a more important role in the model's predictions, both globally and locally.

EBMs have been successfully applied in various domains, such as healthcare and finance, where model transparency and trustworthiness are paramount (Chen et al., 2023; Consiglio, 2023). Their ability to combine state-of-the-art predictive performance with interpretability has made them appealing for high-stakes decision-making. In the context of language learning research, EBMs offer the opportunity to gain insights from the data which would not be possible using deep learning or large ensemble methods due to their complex decision-making processes. By contrast, EBMs facilitate the attribution of model decisions to specific linguistic features.

In this study, the balanced dataset obtained after clustering-based downsampling served as the data for our EBM training. In the preprocessing stage, the variable *Proficiency* was specified as an ordinal categorical feature while the linguistic complexity measures were treated as continuous. As interactions between proficiency and other complexity features may reveal developmental patterns influenced by the SL, a set of pairwise interactions involving *Proficiency* and each complexity feature was explicitly specified. These interactions allowed the EBM to capture how the relationship between linguistic features and the SL differs across proficiency levels. Additionally, as neither complexity measures nor proficiency can validly characterize CLI on their own, all main effects (i.e., standalone complexity measures) were excluded in favor of limiting feature space dimensionality.

Model training was performed using a 5-fold stratified cross-validation procedure through scikit-learn. Each fold involves splitting the data into training and test subsets, training an EBM, as implemented in the InterpretML Python library (Nori et al., 2019) on the training set, and evaluating predictions on the test set. Following cross-validation, overall performance is calculated, and additional analyses are performed to examine performance by proficiency level.

	B1	B2	C1	Total
English	46 (47.4%)	34 (35.1%)	17 (17.5%)	97 (100%)
German	46 (47.4%)	34 (35.1%)	17 (17.5%)	97 (100%)

Table 4: Distribution of texts by SL and CEFR proficiency level after performing clustering-based downsampling.

After confirming the model's stability and predictive power using 5-fold cross-validation, the EBM was retrained on the entire balanced dataset. This final model facilitated the extraction of global feature importance measures. By interpreting these outputs, we were able to identify which complexity features at which proficiency levels best discriminate between HL texts produced by learners from different SLs.

4 Results and Discussion

The EBM trained on the balanced subset of texts achieved a mean accuracy of 0.77 (±0.08) and a mean F1 score of 0.78 (±0.08) in 5-fold cross-validation, substantially above the random guess baseline of 0.5. Additionally, the model achieved a precision score of 0.76 (±0.06) and a recall score of 0.80 (±0.12). These performance metrics lend support to the SL influencing the characterization of HL output. Furthermore, analyzing the performance of the model at each proficiency level revealed that the best performance was achieved at level C1 (Table 5), indicating that SL-driven divergences in complexity features become more pronounced as learners' HL proficiency develops, possibly as a result of formal education in the SL.

	Accuracy	Precision	Recall	F1
B1	0.77	0.76	0.80	0.78
B2	0.75	0.73	0.79	0.76
C1	0.82	0.82	0.82	0.82

Table 5: Model performance by proficiency level based on out-of-fold predictions.

Extracting the most important features for EBM's distinction between the two SLs revealed potential traces of CLI across different linguistic domains (Table 6). However, to determine whether a group of linguistic features on average contributed more to the performance of the model, average feature importance for each class of features was calculated (Table 7), which revealed the greater role of morphological and lexical features, compared to the other classes.

To zoom in on how these two groups of fea-

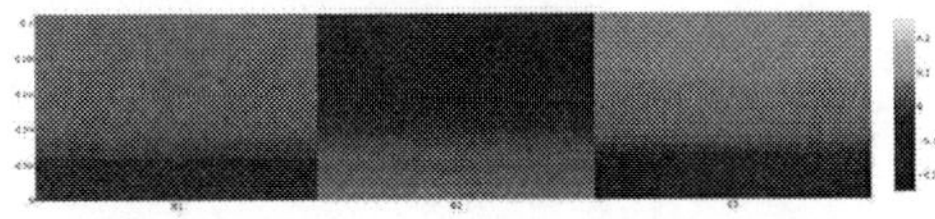

(a) Portuguese Vocabulary Profile (B1)

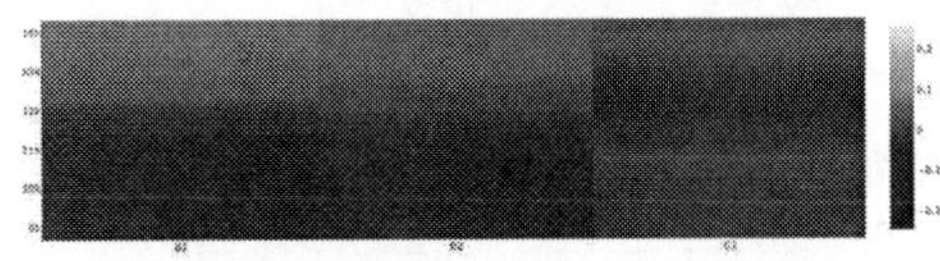

(b) SUBTLEX Word Frequency (SD AW)

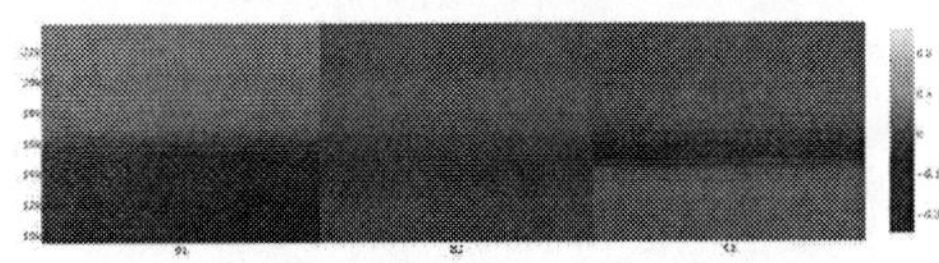

(c) SUBTLEX Word Frequency (FW)

(d) SUBTLEX Contextual Diversity (FW)

Figure 1: Partial plots for the top four lexical features. Darker shades indicate a higher predicted likelihood of German as SL while lighter shades indicate a higher predicted likelihood of English as the SL. The figures have been post-processed for colorblind-friendliness; the original images are available in the study's OSF repository.

Feature	Category
Irregular Verbs in Imperfect Indicative (per verb token)	Grammatical
SUBTLEX Contextual Diversity (FW Token)	Lexical
Portuguese Vocabulary Profile (B1)	Lexical
Regular Verbs in Simple Past Indicative (per verb token)	Grammatical
Imperfect Tense (per verb token)	Morphological
SUBTLEX Word Frequency (SD AW Token)	Lexical
Number of Irregular Verbs in Imperfect Indicative	Count-based
SUBTLEX Word Frequency (FW Token)	Lexical
Infinitive Nominal Subordinate Clauses with Optative and Volitive Verbs	Count-based
SUBTLEX Word Frequency (SD FW Token)	Lexical
Difficult Connectives (per token)	Discursive
First Person (per word token)	Morphological
SUBTLEX Logarithmic Contextual Diversity (FW Token)	Lexical
Number of Agent Modifiers	Count-based
SD of Global Noun Overlap (lemma-based)	Discursive
Regular Verbs in Imperfect Indicative (per verb token)	Grammatical
Punctuation Density	Syntactic
Passive Verbs (per verb token)	Morphological
SUBTLEX Frequency Top 5000	Lexical
SUBTLEX Frequency Band 4	Lexical

Table 6: Top 20 most important features for the EBM model.

Class	Count-based	Lexical	Syntactic	Discursive	Morphological	Grammatical
Importance	13.47%	20.34%	15.64%	18.87%	21.32%	10.37%

Table 7: Average feature class importance.

tures can capture possible CLI in texts produced by English- and German-speaking HL Portuguese learners, we took advantage of the additive structure of EBMs to visualize how specific features contribute to the prediction of the model (Figure 1). While distinct patterns in the top lexical complexity features for each SL are visible across proficiency classes, these differences seem to wane and become less pronounced as learners become more proficient, particularly visible in Figures 1b and 1d. This phenomenon could be indicative of the regularizing effect of higher proficiency on lexical choice in HL learners of different SLs. This assertion is consistent with English-speaking HL learners of Portuguese possibly leveraging cognates of the two languages in the earlier stages of development resulting in higher standard deviation of word frequency for all words (Figure 1b), a measure of linguistic diversity. Similarly, the sudden surge at level B2 and the subsequent drop at level C1 of the use of words characteristic of L2 textbooks at level B1 (Torigoe, 2017) by German-speaking learners (Figure 1a) is suggestive of different developmental trajectories among HL learners with distinct SLs.

We also visualized the contribution of the top morphological features to the model's predictions at each proficiency level (Figure 2). Similar to the patterns observed in lexical complexity features, there are distinct morphological preferences that appear to align with the learner's SL. For instance, English-speaking HL learners consistently exhibit a higher tendency to employ the passive voice across all proficiency levels, with the distinction between the two groups of learners regarding this feature becoming more pronounced at the C1 level (Figure 2c). This pattern may be explained by the structural similarity of the passive voice in English and Portuguese, as opposed to German, making it more accessible to learners whose SL is English. In contrast, German-speaking HL learners show a clear preference for using the imperfect tense and the first person as they become more proficient (Figures 2a and 2b). The preference for the imperfect tense among German-speaking learners may stem from the presence of a comparable tense form in German, facilitating its transfer into Portuguese. The inclination toward first-person constructions by German-speaking learners could similarly be interpreted as consistent with their lack of preference for the passive voice. In contrast to lexical features which showed a tendency to converge as learners from distinct SLs become more proficient in their HL, the influence of morphosyntactic features follow the opposite trend, with learners' HL appearing to be influenced more heavily by the morphosyntactic properties of the SL at more advanced levels. An explanation for this could be that as learners progress through their HL classes, the SL, as their dominant language, also continues to become more entrenched as a result of formal education in the SL.

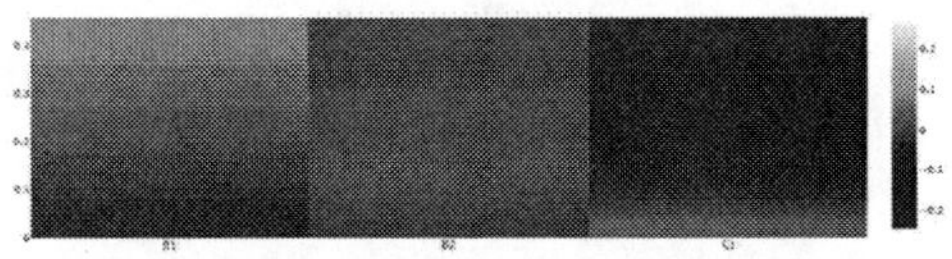

(a) Imperfect tense (per verb token)

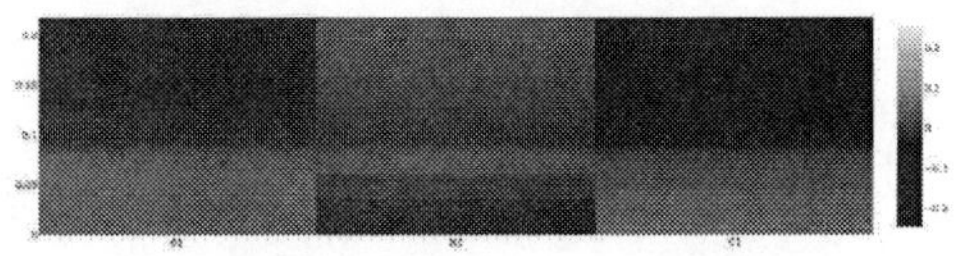

(b) First Person (per word token)

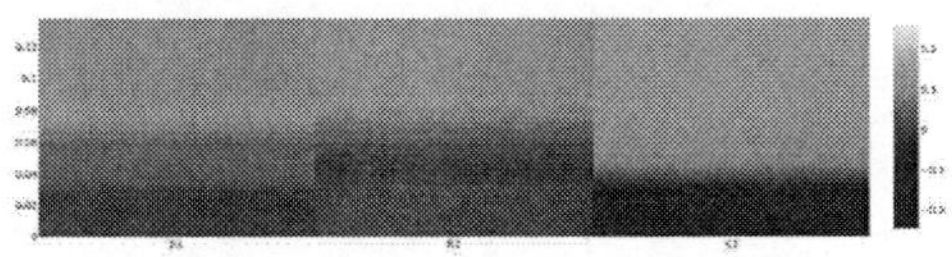

(c) Passive verbs (per verb token)

Figure 2: Partial plots for the top three morphological features. Darker shades indicate a higher predicted likelihood of German as SL while lighter shades indicate a higher predicted likelihood of English as the SL. The figures have been post-processed for colorblind-friendliness; the original images are available in the study's OSF repository.

5 Conclusion

This study set out to explore CLI in HL learners of Portuguese by examining how the SL shapes patterns of lexical and morphosyntactic use, following the detection-based approach to CLI research (Jarvis, 2010). While our findings highlight certain trends, particularly with regard to lexical and morphological preferences, it is important to recognize that due to the exploratory nature of the study, these results offer only one perspective within a broader landscape of theoretical and empirical approaches. Rather than provide a definitive characterization of CLI in the context of HL, our aim was to explore how data-driven approaches, specifically interpretable machine learning, can be utilized to conduct scientific inquiry into CLI. Through more extensive datasets, more detailed typological comparisons, and closer engagement with CLI theory, subsequent investigations can refine our understanding of CLI, allowing us to move beyond preliminary evidence toward a richer, more comprehensive account of how the SL shapes the evolving linguistic knowledge of HL learners.

Acknowledgments

This work was developed within the scope of the project *Promoção da Aquisição e ensino do Português como Língua de Herança através de Ferramentas Digitais Inteligentes*, financed by the Foundation for Science and Technology - FCT of the Republic of Portugal and the Camões Institute. We would like to thank anonymous reviewers for their insightful comments on a previous version of this paper.

References

Soroosh Akef, Amália Mendes, Detmar Meurers, and Patrick Rebuschat. 2024. Investigating the generalizability of Portuguese readability assessment models trained using linguistic complexity features. In *Proceedings of the 16th International Conference on Computational Processing of Portuguese - Vol. 1*, pages 332–341, Santiago de Compostela, Galicia/Spain. Association for Computational Lingustics.

Luiz Amaral and Detmar Meurers. 2008. From recording linguistic competence to supporting inferences about language acquisition in context: Extending the conceptualization of student models for intelligent computer-assisted language learning. *Computer-Assisted Language Learning*, 21(4):323–338.

Fatih Bayram, Jason Rothman, Michael Iverson, Tanja Kupisch, David Miller, Eloi Puig-Mayenco, and Marit Westergaard. 2019. Differences in use without deficiencies in competence: passives in the Turkish and German of Turkish heritage speakers in Germany. *International Journal of Bilingual Education and Bilingualism*, 22(8):919–939. Publisher: Routledge _eprint: https://doi.org/10.1080/13670050.2017.1324403.

Elabbas Benmamoun, Silvina Montrul, and Maria Polinsky. 2013. Heritage languages and their speakers: Opportunities and challenges for linguistics. *Theoretical Linguistics*, 39(3-4):129–181.

Rupal Bhargava, Jaspreet Singh, Shivangi Arora, and Yashvardhan Sharma. 2017. Bits_pilani@inli-fire-2017: Indian native language identification using deep learning. In *FIRE*.

David M. Blei, Andrew Y. Ng, and Michael I. Jordan. 2003. Latent dirichlet allocation. *J. Mach. Learn. Res.*, 3(null):993–1022.

Bernhard Brehmer and Irina Usanova. 2015. Lets fix it? In *Transfer Effects in Multilingual Language Development*, pages 161–188. John Benjamins.

Bram Bulté, Alex Housen, and Gabriele Pallotti. 2024. Complexity and difficulty in second language acquisition: A theoretical and methodological overview. *Language Learning*.

Bram Bulté and Alex Housen. 2012. Defining and operationalising L2 complexity. In Alex Housen, Folkert Kuiken, and Ineke Vedder, editors, *Dimensions of L2 Performance and Proficiency*, Language Learning & Language Teaching, pages 21–46. John Benjamins Publishing Company, Amsterdam.

Serhiy Bykh and Detmar Meurers. 2014. Exploring syntactic features for native language identification: A variationist perspective on feature encoding and ensemble optimization. In *Proceedings of COLING 2014, the 25th International Conference on Computational Linguistics: Technical Papers*, pages 1962–1973, Dublin, Ireland. Dublin City University and Association for Computational Linguistics.

Serhiy Bykh and Detmar Meurers. 2016. Advancing linguistic features and insights by label-informed feature grouping: An exploration in the context of native language identification. In *Proceedings of COLING 2016, the 26th International Conference on Computational Linguistics: Technical Papers*, pages 739–749, Osaka, Japan. The COLING 2016 Organizing Committee.

Serhiy Bykh, Sowmya Vajjala, Julia Krivanek, and Detmar Meurers. 2013. Combining shallow and linguistically motivated features in native language identification. In *Proceedings of the Eighth Workshop on Innovative Use of NLP for Building Educational Applications*, pages 197–206, Atlanta, Georgia. Association for Computational Linguistics.

Marlene Böttcher and Margaret Zellers. 2024. Do you say uh or uhm? A cross-linguistic approach to filler particle use in heritage and majority speakers across three languages. *Frontiers in Psychology*, 15. Publisher: Frontiers.

Iain Carmichael and J. S. Marron. 2018. Data science vs. statistics: two cultures? *Japanese Journal of Statistics and Data Science*, 1(1):117–138.

Xiaobin Chen and Detmar Meurers. 2016. CTAP: A Web-Based Tool Supporting Automatic Complexity Analysis. In *Proceedings of the Workshop on Computational Linguistics for Linguistic Complexity (CL4LC)*, pages 113–119, Osaka, Japan. The COLING 2016 Organizing Committee.

Zhi Chen, Sarah Tan, Urszula Chajewska, Cynthia Rudin, and Rich Caruana. 2023. Missing Values and Imputation in Healthcare Data: Can Interpretable Machine Learning Help? ArXiv:2304.11749 [cs] version: 1.

Maria Chinkina and Detmar Meurers. 2016. Linguistically aware information retrieval: Providing input enrichment for second language learners. In *Proceedings of the 11th Workshop on Innovative Use of NLP for Building Educational Applications*, pages 188–198, San Diego, CA. Association for Computational Linguistics.

Alessandro Consiglio. 2023. Model interpretability in credit insurance. Master's thesis, Instituto Superior de Economia e Gestão, March. Accepted: 2023-03-24T13:57:00Z.

Council of Europe. 2001. Common European Framework of References for Languages: Learning, teachning, assessment.

Alejandro Cuza. 2013. Crosslinguistic influence at the syntax proper: Interrogative subject–verb inversion in heritage Spanish. *International Journal of Bilingualism*, 17(1):71–96. Publisher: SAGE Publications Ltd.

Eric Demattos. 2020. Analyzing linguistic complexity of l2 portuguese for automatic proficiency classification. Master's thesis, Eberhard Karls University of Tübingen.

Rod Ellis and Gary Barkhuizen. 2005. *Analysing Learner Language*. Oxford University Press.

Cristina Flores and Pilar Barbosa. 2014. When reduced input leads to delayed acquisition: A study on the acquisition of clitic placement by portuguese heritage speakers. *International Journal of Bilingualism*, 18(3):304–325.

Clara Fridman, Maria Polinsky, and Natalia Meir. 2024. Cross-linguistic influence meets diminished input: A comparative study of heritage Russian in contact with Hebrew and English. *Second Language Research*, 40(3):675–708. Publisher: SAGE Publications Ltd.

Sidney Gordon and Natalia Meir. 2024. English as a heritage language: The effects of input patterns and contact with Hebrew. *International Journal of Bilingualism*, 28(3):353–373. Publisher: SAGE Publications Ltd.

Dhiman Goswami, Sharanya Thilagan, Kai North, Shervin Malmasi, and Marcos Zampieri. 2024. Native language identification in texts: A survey. In

Proceedings of the 2024 Conference of the North American Chapter of the Association for Computational Linguistics: Human Language Technologies (Volume 1: Long Papers), pages 3149–3160, Mexico City, Mexico. Association for Computational Linguistics.

John A. Hawkins and Paula Buttery. 2010. Criterial Features in Learner Corpora: Theory and Illustrations. *English Profile Journal*, 1:e5.

Matthew Honnibal, Ines Montani, Sofie Van Landeghem, and Adriane Boyd. 2020. spaCy: Industrial-strength Natural Language Processing in Python.

Scott Jarvis. 2010. Comparison-based and detection-based approaches to transfer research. *EUROSLA Yearbook*, 10(1):169–192.

Wei-Chao Lin, Chih-Fong Tsai, Ya-Han Hu, and Jing-Shang Jhang. 2017. Clustering-based undersampling in class-imbalanced data. *Information Sciences*, 409-410:17–26.

Anand Kumar M, Barathi Ganesh H. B., Ajay S. G, and Soman K. P. 2018. Overview of the second shared task on indian native language identification (INLI). In *Working Notes of FIRE 2018 - Forum for Information Retrieval Evaluation, Gandhinagar, India, December 6-9, 2018*, volume 2266 of *CEUR Workshop Proceedings*, pages 39–50. CEUR-WS.org.

Brian Macwhinney. 1987. *The Competition Model*, pages 249–308. Lawrence Erlbaum.

Shervin Malmasi and Mark Dras. 2014. Finnish native language identification. In *Proceedings of the Australasian Language Technology Association Workshop 2014*, pages 139–144, Melbourne, Australia.

Shervin Malmasi and Mark Dras. 2018. Native language identification with classifier stacking and ensembles. *Computational Linguistics*, 44(3):403–446.

Shervin Malmasi, Keelan Evanini, Aoife Cahill, Joel Tetreault, Robert Pugh, Christopher Hamill, Diane Napolitano, and Yao Qian. 2017. A report on the 2017 native language identification shared task. In *Proceedings of the 12th Workshop on Innovative Use of NLP for Building Educational Applications*, pages 62–75, Copenhagen, Denmark. Association for Computational Linguistics.

Kevin McManus. 2019. Awareness of L1 form-meaning mappings can reduce crosslinguistic effects in L2 grammatical learning. *Language Awareness*, 28(2):114–138.

Kevin McManus. 2021. *Crosslinguistic Influence and Second Language Learning*. Routledge, New York.

Natalia Meir and Bibi Janssen. 2021. Child Heritage Language Development: An Interplay Between Cross-Linguistic Influence and Language-External Factors. *Frontiers in Psychology*, 12. Publisher: Frontiers.

Detmar Meurers, Ramon Ziai, Luiz Amaral, Adriane Boyd, Aleksandar Dimitrov, Vanessa Metcalf, and Niels Ott. 2010. Enhancing authentic web pages for language learners. In *Proceedings of the NAACL HLT 2010 Fifth Workshop on Innovative Use of NLP for Building Educational Applications*, pages 10–18, Los Angeles, California. Association for Computational Linguistics.

David Mimno, Hanna Wallach, Edmund Talley, Miriam Leenders, and Andrew McCallum. 2011. Optimizing semantic coherence in topic models. In *Proceedings of the 2011 Conference on Empirical Methods in Natural Language Processing*, pages 262–272, Edinburgh, Scotland, UK. Association for Computational Linguistics.

Elham Mohammadi, Hadi Veisi, and Hessam Amini. 2017. Native language identification using a mixture of character and word n-grams. In *Proceedings of the 12th Workshop on Innovative Use of NLP for Building Educational Applications*, pages 210–216, Copenhagen, Denmark. Association for Computational Linguistics.

Rajesh Kumar Mundotiya, Manish Singh, and Anil Kumar Singh. 2018. Nlprl@inli-2018: Hybrid gated lstm-cnn model for indian native language identification. In *FIRE*.

W. James Murdoch, Chandan Singh, Karl Kumbier, Reza Abbasi-Asl, and Bin Yu. 2019. Definitions, methods, and applications in interpretable machine learning. *Proceedings of the National Academy of Sciences*, 116(44):22071–22080.

Harsha Nori, Samuel Jenkins, Paul Koch, and Rich Caruana. 2019. Interpretml: A unified framework for machine learning interpretability. *arXiv preprint arXiv:1909.09223*.

Terence Odlin. 2022. *Explorations of Language Transfer*. Multilingual Matters, Bristol, Blue Ridge Summit.

Brechje van Osch. 2019. Vulnerability and cross-linguistic influence in heritage spanish: Comparing different majority languages. *Heritage Language Journal*, 16(3):340 – 366.

Gabriele Pallotti. 2015. A simple view of linguistic complexity. *Second Language Research*, 31(1):117–134. Publisher: SAGE Publications Ltd.

Fabian Pedregosa, Gaël Varoquaux, Alexandre Gramfort, Vincent Michel, Bertrand Thirion, Olivier Grisel, Mathieu Blondel, Andreas Müller, Joel Nothman, Gilles Louppe, Peter Prettenhofer, Ron Weiss, Vincent Dubourg, Jake Vanderplas, Alexandre Passos, David Cournapeau, Matthieu Brucher, Matthieu Perrot, and Édouard Duchesnay. 2018. Scikit-learn: Machine learning in python.

Radim Řehůřek and Petr Sojka. 2010. Software Framework for Topic Modelling with Large Corpora. In

Proceedings of the LREC 2010 Workshop on New Challenges for NLP Frameworks, pages 45–50, Valletta, Malta. ELRA.

Luisa Ribeiro-Flucht, Xiaobin Chen, and Detmar Meurers. 2024. Explainable AI in language learning: Linking empirical evidence and theoretical concepts in proficiency and readability modeling of Portuguese. In *Proceedings of the 19th Workshop on Innovative Use of NLP for Building Educational Applications (BEA 2024)*, pages 199–209, Mexico City, Mexico. Association for Computational Linguistics.

Jason Rothman, Fatih Bayram, Vincent DeLuca, Grazia Di Pisa, Jon Andoni Duñabeitia, Khadij Gharibi, Jiuzhou Hao, Nadine Kolb, Maki Kubota, Tanja Kupisch, Tim Laméris, Alicia Luque, Brechje van Osch, Sergio Miguel Pereira Soares, Yanina Prystauka, Deniz Tat, Aleksandra Tomić, Toms Voits, and Stefanie Wulff. 2023. Monolingual comparative normativity in bilingualism research is out of "control": Arguments and alternatives. *Applied Psycholinguistics*, 44(3):316–329.

Richard W. Schmidt. 1990. The role of consciousness in second language learning1. *Applied Linguistics*, 11(2):129–158.

Gregory Scontras, Zuzanna Fuchs, and Maria Polinsky. 2015. Heritage language and linguistic theory. *Frontiers in Psychology*, 6. Publisher: Frontiers.

Yuhyeon Seo and Alejandro Cuza. 2024. On the production of bare nouns and case marking in Korean heritage speakers in contact with English. *Lingua*, 311:103826.

Joel Tetreault, Daniel Blanchard, and Aoife Cahill. 2013. A report on the first native language identification shared task. In *Proceedings of the Eighth Workshop on Innovative Use of NLP for Building Educational Applications*, pages 48–57, Atlanta, Georgia. Association for Computational Linguistics.

Shintaro Torigoe. 2017. Portuguese Vocabulary Profile: uma lista de vocabulário a aprendentes do PL2/PLE, baseada nos corpora de aprendentes e de livros de ensino. *Revista da Associação Portuguesa de Linguística*, 3:387–400.

Jacopo Torregrossa, Cristina Flores, and Esther Rinke. 2023. What modulates the acquisition of difficult structures in a heritage language? a study on portuguese in contact with french, german and italian. *Bilingualism: Language and Cognition*, 26(1):179–192.

Sowmya Vajjala and Sagnik Banerjee. 2017. A study of n-gram and embedding representations for native language identification. In *Proceedings of the 12th Workshop on Innovative Use of NLP for Building Educational Applications*, pages 240–248, Copenhagen, Denmark. Association for Computational Linguistics.

Tatiana Verkhovtceva, Maria Polinsky, and Natalia Meir. 2023. Cross-linguistic influence, limited input, or working-memory limitations: The morphosyntax of agreement and concord in Heritage Russian. *Applied Psycholinguistics*, 44(5):941–968.

Zarah Weiss and Detmar Meurers. 2019. Analyzing linguistic complexity and accuracy in academic language development of German across elementary and secondary school. In *Proceedings of the Fourteenth Workshop on Innovative Use of NLP for Building Educational Applications*, pages 380–393, Florence, Italy. Association for Computational Linguistics.

Kathryn Elizabeth Wolfe-Quintero. 1998. *Second language development in writing : measures of fluency, accuracy, & complexity*. University of Hawai'i, Second Language Teaching & Curriculum Center.

Wei Zhang and Alexandre Salle. 2023. Native Language Identification with Large Language Models. ArXiv:2312.07819 [cs].

A prototype authoring tool for editing authentic texts using LLMs to increase support for contextualised L2 grammar practice

Stephen Bodnar
Tübingen Center for Digital Education, University of Tübingen, Germany
stephen.bodnar@uni-tuebingen.de

Abstract

ICALL systems that offer grammar exercises with authentic texts have the potential to motivate learners, but finding suitable documents can be problematic because of the low number of target grammar forms they typically contain. Meanwhile, research showing the ability of Large Language Models (LLMs) to rewrite texts in controlled ways is emerging, and this begs the question of whether or not they can be used to modify authentic L2 texts to increase their suitability for grammar learning. In this paper we present a tool we have developed to explore this idea.The authoring tool employs a lexical database to create prompts that instruct an LLM to insert specific target forms into the text. We share our plans to evaluate the quality of the automatically modified texts based on human judgments from native speakers.

1 Introduction

Perhaps because learning grammar is sometimes perceived as boring by students (e.g., Jean and Simard, 2011), researchers have explored a variety of techniques for spicing up computerised grammar practice. For example, Colling et al. (2024) developed a student dashboard that highlighted the relevance of practice exercises to communicative tasks. Adding gamification elements to make grammar practice more exciting or enjoyable is another possibility (Strik et al., 2013). Occasionally researchers develop speech-interactive grammar practice to help develop oral proficiency (Drozdova et al., 2013). Still another approach is to contextualise the practice by situating it within an interesting mystery narrative (Cornillie et al., 2013). The work we present here connects with previous work in Intelligent Computer-Assisted Language Learning (ICALL) that contextualises grammar practice through the use of authentic texts (e.g., Meurers, Ziai, Amaral, Boyd, Dimitrov, Metcalf, and Ott 2010).

In the next section we draw on the instructed L2 learning literature to build a case for why and how authentic texts can be used to contextualise grammar practice. Next, we review past work in ICALL that uses authentic texts to deliver grammar practice. We then discuss some of the challenges with using authentic texts for grammar practice, and follow by suggesting that LLMs as a tool for rewriting texts may be effective for increasing the availability of authentic texts suitable for grammar practice. Section 3 outlines a high-level method for using LLMs to increase the number of target linguistic forms in a document. In Section 4, we present an authoring tool we have developed that employs this method to support L2 French instruction targeting grammatical gender and gender-predictive noun suffixes. Section 5 presents our plans to evaluate the method and tool, and in Section 6 we discuss current limitations with our proposal.

2 Background

2.1 Authentic texts in grammar instruction - why and how ?

Pedagogically speaking, the use of authentic texts[1] as contexts for grammar practice is interesting for both compelling motivational and linguistic reasons.

One frequently given reason is related to motivation. In their survey of authentic materials in foreign language learning, Gilmore (2007) lists

[1] As Gilmore points out, the term 'authentic' has been defined differently in the literature, and depending on the researcher can include or exclude text that has been modified for educational purposes. In the present paper, we follow Gillmore (2007) and adopt Morrow's (1977) definition, i.e. authentic material is "a stretch of real language, produced by a real speaker or writer for a real audience and designed to convey a real message of some sort" (p.13) and may include texts modified for instructional purposes.

Stephen Bodnar. A prototype authoring tool for editing authentic texts using LLMs to increase support for contextualised L2 grammar practice. *Proceedings of the 14th Workshop on Natural Language Processing for Computer Assisted Language Learning (NLP4CALL 2025)*. University of Tartu Library. 63–71.

some of the more common rationales: authentic texts are inherently more interesting because their purpose is "to communicate a message rather than highlight target language" (p. 107); authentic texts are challenging but overcoming the challenges can in itself be motivating; instruction using authentic texts allows more freedom to choose material that matches with specific learner interests; authentic texts can be seen as giving learners an opportunity to leave the sandboxed world of textbooks and work with 'real' material intended for native speakers (see also Berwald, 1987). Although these claims seem plausible, and are compatible with L2 motivation theories (e.g., those related to self-efficacy, self-determination, or Gardner's notion of integrative orientation; see Dörnyei and Ushioda, 2011, pp. 16, 23-25, 41), Gilmore (2007) points out that there is also disagreement in the literature and that few empirical studies exist, leaving the link between authentic materials and motivation as an important area for future work.

Turning to linguistic reasons for using authentic texts, from a perspective focused on grammar learning, a well-chosen authentic text can serve as a good basis for providing the essential ingredients for acquiring new grammar knowledge through practice. First, exposure to relevant L2 input, in this case target language grammar forms, is available from the text, and can be combined with input enhancement techniques (e.g., highlighting) to help learners notice specific word forms and linguistic structures[2] (Ziegler et al., 2017). Second, opportunities to produce L2 output can be made available by drawing on the text to create written or spoken grammar activities in the classroom (e.g., Lyster, 2018) or computerised self-study (see Section 2.2). These exercises in turn serve as opportunities for learners to receive corrective feedback on their output to push them to develop their linguistic accuracy.

From a more holistic instructional perspective, it is important to point out that these opportunities for L2 input and output practice take place within a meaningful context, i.e. the authentic text whose main purpose is to communicate a message. Combining content and grammar practice together helps to ensure that both communication and linguistic accuracy goals receive support and neither is left behind (Lyster, 2018).

Unfortunately, practical constraints often stand in the way of implementing the kind of contextualised grammar practice described above. When the focus of instruction is on meaning and attention to grammar is given incidentally, for example in response to questions from learners, instruction can take place without special attention to the linguistic structures present in a text. However, to support instruction with specific grammar learning goals, what is needed are texts featuring many instances of specific linguistic structures, which is possible but can be challenging (see Section 2.2.2). Another practical issue is that, unlike textbook material, authentic texts do not come with the accompanying comprehension and grammar practice exercises. These additional materials can be developed by instructors or material developers, but it is of course extra work. In the next section we review research efforts aimed at developing technology that makes it easier to use authentic texts in grammar instruction.

2.2 ICALL systems supporting grammar practice with authentic texts

2.2.1 Existing systems

ICALL tools targeting grammar practice with authentic texts tend to provide support for one of two tasks, namely 1) helping to find suitable texts and 2) creating accompanying exercise sets.

Tools that help with finding suitable texts combine automated linguistic profilers with search interfaces (e.g., Hagiwara et al., 2021; Dittrich et al., 2019; Chinkina and Meurers, 2016). The linguistic profilers use NLP pipelines to analyze documents and obtain fine-grained information such as how frequently different POS tags, verb tenses, clause types, and other grammatical phenomena appear in a text. The search interfaces allow users to locate documents based on keywords and desired linguistic criteria. For example, in FLAIR (Chinkina and Meurers, 2016) users can specify that they are interested in documents related to the keyword 'weekend' that also feature verbs in the simple past or which contain Wh- questions. Search interfaces often use highlighting to help users quickly locate strings in the document that satisfy their search criteria, and in this way get an indication of how useful a text is for teaching particular linguistic structures. The tools target differ-

[2] Similar to (Ziegler et al., 2017), we use the term 'linguistic structure' to refer to abstract grammatical structures (e.g., a noun phrase consisting of a determiner and noun), and the term 'form' to refer to surface language instances of these structures (e.g., *a bicycle*, *un vélo*).

ent languages, with FLAIR (Chinkina and Meurers, 2016) supporting English, Octanove Learn supporting English and Chinese (Hagiwara et al., 2021), and KANSAS targeting German (Dittrich et al., 2019). Often these tools include information on the CEFR level to give a global characterisation of the L2 proficiency range a text is suitable for.

A larger number of systems have been developed that accept authentic text as input and create accompanying exercises. A helpful observation made by Heck and Meurers (2022) is that these systems use the authentic material in mainly two different ways. On the one hand, there are systems that in a sense mine the authentic material to identify seed sentences, and transform these into individual, stand-alone exercise or test items where the larger meaningful context surrounding the exercise is discarded, and the meaningful context is limited to the item itself (e.g. Baptista et al., 2016; Chalvin et al., 2013; Aldabe et al., 2006). On the other hand, there are systems that aim to leave the authentic material intact and present it to learners as one coherent whole and integrate grammar exercises into the text presentation and thereby make it interactive.

The distinction between limited-context and full-context systems is important because it helps us see that it is the latter full-context systems that best align with instructional methods that push learners to attend to meaning and form (see Section 2.1).

A prominent example of a full-context system is the *Working with English Real Texts interactively* (WeRTi) tool that transforms web texts into an interactive web page where parts of the original document become different kinds of interactive practice items, for example fill-in-the-blank items (Meurers et al., 2010). A number of other full-context systems have been developed, including a browser plugin called VIEW for Russian (Reynolds et al., 2014) and North Saami (Antonsen and Argese, 2018), the Language Muse Activity Palette (Burstein et al., 2017) and the AGREE system (Chan et al., 2022) for English , the COLLIE e-learning platform targeting French (Bodnar, 2022), and an extension of FLAIR that adds exercise generation features (Heck and Meurers, 2022).

Summarising, ICALL researchers have developed a number of innovative search and exercise generation tools that help lower the barrier to creating full-context grammar exercises that offer both L2 input and output practice. Some of these tools are freely available online, which is an important step for more wide-spread adoption that can help the field to make a real-world impact on L2 instruction, as well as inspire the development of new tools that target so-far unsupported languages.

2.2.2 Challenges with using authentic text

Arguments against using authentic texts have been presented in the literature on automatic exercise generation, but the points are not so much critiques of the instructional validity or usefulness of full-context systems but instead more related to practical difficulties. One common point is that authentic materials such as language corpora often do not naturally contain a sufficient number or variety of target linguistic structures (Aldabe et al., 2006). A second point is that the sentences in authentic materials can be very complex and more suitable for intermediate and advanced learners (Perez-Beltrachini et al., 2012).

In a nutshell, these views are arguing that finding suitable material to support contextualised grammar practice is difficult. This can be for at least two reasons, either suitable documents exist but are difficult to find, or suitable documents are very rare. For the former, certainly tools like FLAIR can be helpful for locating relevant documents if they exist. However, based on our own recent experience crawling RSS feeds to build a database of documents suitable for practising French grammatical gender, we would tend to agree with others that documents that are naturally suitable for grammar instruction targeting specific word forms or structures can be rare, and in this case linguistically-aware search tools unfortunately do not have much to offer.

One way to handle this problem is to adopt a more pragmatic perspective and aim for a compromise in which we accept that only stand-alone practice items are feasible, but when creating them try to include as much context as possible. An advantage of this approach is that we are no longer constrained to text from the same document; instead, the systems are free to search through multiple documents and cherry pick, producing more practice items and opportunities for learners.

Another way to handle this problem is to consider editing authentic texts to make them more suitable, by for example, carefully introducing instances of target grammar forms that will be the focus of a lesson. To our knowledge no tool exists that helps authors adapt an existing text to make it more suitable for grammar practice. While costly, employing human authors to edit a text to, for example, include more pedagogically desirable linguistic structures is possible. However, clearly some form of technological support that lowers the barrier to contextualising grammar practice with authentic texts would be welcome.

2.3 LLMs as a tool for rewriting texts to support grammar practice

Interest in how LLMs can be used to perform useful everyday tasks has increased in recent years (Yang et al., 2024), with some researchers exploring their potential for editing or rewriting text (Shu et al., 2024). In one study, researchers working in the area of search advertising have begun to investigate whether or not LLMs can rewrite texts to blend in advertisements into chatbot responses so that they appear seamlessly, a technique known as native advertising (Zelch et al., 2024).

The impressive capabilities of LLMs and in particular the emerging findings that LLMs can be effective tools for rewriting beg the question of whether or not an LLM approach could be used to address some of the challenges with using authentic texts for grammar instruction discussed above (see Section 2.2.2). These abilities suggest that LLMs might be able to modify authentic texts to make them more pedagogically useful. Such an approach would need to find a balance between maintaining the authenticity of the text as much as as possible, while inserting or substituting target linguistic forms into the text, and possibly deleting sections of text, to seamlessly blend in the modifications. Doing so would require developing prompts that instruct an LLM to perform the needed edits, and measures (automatic or human judgements) for determining the degree to which a modified text has been improved. In the next section we propose a method for using LLMs to edit authentic texts to support grammar practice.

3 Proposed method

We assume that the input is an authentic L2 text t an instructor would like to use (e.g., because it is on an interesting topic) for providing practice on a specific linguistic structure s. We also assume that a reference linguistic profile p is available to specify what an ideal document should look like from a linguistic point of view, that is, the number and variety of target forms needed to support learning. Lastly, we assume an LLM service is accessible via a remote API. Then, the procedure we propose consists of four steps:

- Step 1: Profile the input document t to count the number of occurrences of target grammatical forms; compare these with counts in the reference linguistic profile to obtain the difference n.
- Step 2: Generate a set of n target-form strings needed to reduce the difference to zero, where a target form is a surface-language realization, e.g., if the linguistic structure is a verb phrase requiring verbs in the Simple Past, a target form string could be "I went", or "She saw".
- Step 3: Modify an LLM prompt template by inserting instructions to seamlessly blend in each grammatical target string, send the prompt to the LLM API, and store the result.
- Step 4: Profile the rewritten document and compare the resulting text with the reference linguistic profile, and repeat / manually adjust if necessary until n is negligible.

To help make clear how the method would work and what resources other than an LLM are needed, we outline how we are currently using this method in the context of the COLLIE e-learning platform (Bodnar, 2022), which provides instruction on French grammatical gender and includes an exercise generation pipeline.

A prerequisite of the proposed method is a reference linguistic profile. Its purpose is to indicate whether or not COLLIE would be able to generate an exercise with a suitable number of items covering the target structures and including a variety of forms. Specifying these criteria requires pedagogical consideration and should take into account the amount of time available for a lesson and its learning objectives. In our case, we obtain a linguistic profile by processing texts created in a previous human-led instructional intervention with COLLIE's NLP pipeline (see Bodnar, 2022). However, a profile could also be created without a reference document, for example by providing users with a settings panel similar to those used in

ICALL search tools (see Section 2.2.1) that allows users to specify different linguistic criteria.

The profiling stage (Step 1) requires the ability to automatically detect target linguistic structures. In our review in Section 2.2.1 we saw that this technology is already available (e.g., FLAIR). In our case we implement this ability using an NLP pipeline that detects French singular nouns featuring gender-predictive suffixes along with their determiners (e.g., *une potion*, *un bateau*; see Lyster, 2006). The pipeline, implemented in Java, detects these forms using the output of a dependency parser from the Stanford CoreNLP toolkit (Manning et al., 2014) and the *Lexique* database, the latter to ensure that nouns with target suffixes actually have the expected gender (for details, see Bodnar, 2022).

Step 2 above requires some generation capabilities, however, note that the goal here is to generate short strings containing target forms; we rely on the LLM in Step 3 to blend these into the text. To accomplish this, we propose using computational linguistic resources that offer precise control for generating only the needed target forms. In the case of French, *Lexique* (New et al., 2004) is a comprehensive database containing information on grammatical gender for over 45,000 nouns and is freely available; we use this resource to build a list of strings consisting of singular nouns with gender-predictive suffixes preceded by a determiner [3]. For other instructional targets, NLG tools like Simple NLG (Gatt and Reiter, 2009; SimpleNLG) and GramEx (Perez-Beltrachini et al., 2012), or corpus-mining approaches (see Section 2.2.1) could be used to obtain the short strings featuring the target forms.

Step 3 involves selecting an LLM service and developing a suitable prompt template. The LLM service used in the prototype is the OpenAI API platform[4] with the ChatGPT 3.5 Turbo model. Although this is not the most recent model available, it offers competitive performance on rewrite tasks (Shu et al., 2024). Based on our experience with the prompt shown in Figure 1, the model appears to perform well enough to be used in the prototype, and it has the advantage of being relatively inexpensive, which is important during tool development, when testing new features and fixing bugs require many API calls. Clearly, however, different LLM models and prompt formulations are parameters that should be explored in a future evaluation.

```
Please rewrite the text below to include the string
    'la cuisine'.
Also please rewrite the text below to include the string
    'une chose'.
...
Also please rewrite the text below to include the string
    'un bateau'.
Please combine the rewrites into one coherent text.
Text: <TEXT>
```

Figure 1: An example of the current LLM prompt template we are using.

In Step 4, content authors examine the output from the LLM and decide whether or not the result is satisfactory. We assume that the success of the LLM-performed edits will vary, and that an iterative workflow will be necessary (see Figure 2).

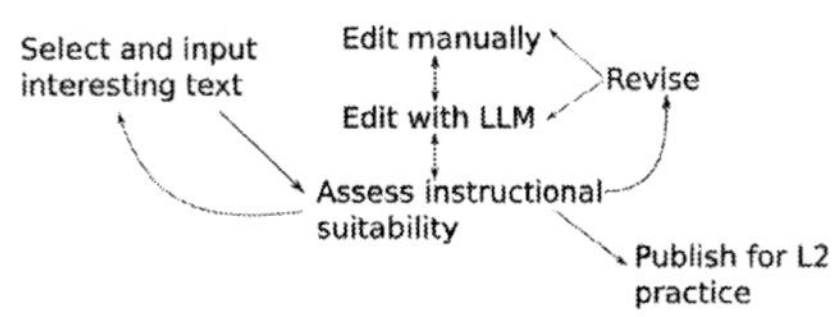

Figure 2: Authoring workflow with an LLM-enhanced authoring tool.

Comparing longer documents manually would be tedious and a productivity bottleneck. In the next section we present an authoring tool we have developed to support users during potentially multiple rounds of document modification.

4 Authoring tool prototype for French grammar practice

To explore the method described in Section 3 we have implemented a prototype authoring tool designed to assist authors with editing authentic texts to better support instruction targeting specific grammatical phenomena. The tool combines the linguistic profiling of ICALL search tools (see Section 2.2) with a prompt generation feature that makes it easy to generate specific instructions that can be used by an LLM to insert target forms into an authentic text. The tool incorporates dashboard-inspired visual elements so that authors can quickly assess the status of the documents in their collection. Figure 3 shows the current user interface.

[3] The current implementation selects nouns based on their suffixes without consideration of semantic fit; implementing a semantic fit criterion and investigating its impact on the quality of edited texts would be an interesting future direction.

[4] https://platform.openai.com/

The left pane shows the documents in the author's collection. Each document is displayed with bar graphs that indicate the readiness of a document for supporting a specific grammar instruction target. Colors communicate a document's status, with green bars indicating that a criterion has been met, and blue that more work is needed. The first two bars show the number of words in the text and the number of target forms, both relative to a desired value specified in the reference linguistic profile. The third bar provides a measure of a document's support for practice with a variety of target structures. We define this score, which we refer to as the "**c**overage of **t**arget **s**tructures" or *cts* score, for a document *d* and a set of target linguistic structures *s*, as

$$cts(d) = \frac{\sum_{i=1}^{len(s)} min(\frac{num\_target\_forms_i}{des\_num\_target\_forms_i}, 1)}{len(s)}$$

where *len(s)* is the number of distinct linguistic structures to practice in the lesson, $num\_target\_forms_i$ is the number of forms found in the document for the *i*th target linguistic structure, and $des\_num\_target\_forms_i$ is the desired number of forms for the *i*th target linguistic structure specified in the reference linguistic profile.

To give a concrete example using grammatical gender with predictive suffixes, a lesson may ask a student to practice forming noun phrases with single nouns featuring the three suffixes *-tion* (typically feminine), and *-eau* and *-age* (typically masculine). In this case, a document should score well when each of the suffixes are present in the document with the needed counts (defined in the reference linguistic profile), and no one suffix that happens to frequently occur should be allowed to compensate for other suffixes that are lacking.

The right pane is where an author can work on a text to make it more suitable for grammar instruction. Fine-grained information for each of the structures a learner should practice is available using the same bar graph format, again with target thresholds for criteria values (target word count, number of items, and number of instances of noun phrases for each gender-predictive suffix) set from the reference linguistic profile. Using these, an author can quickly understand the strengths and weakness of the document.

The tool provides authors with support in addressing weaknesses in the document by making available the method proposed in Section 3. Authors can generate an LLM prompt with a button click; the prompt can be modified before being sent to the remote LLM service. Once received, the generated text is saved to a database and tagged with a new version, in case a rollback is needed. The document text can also be edited manually.

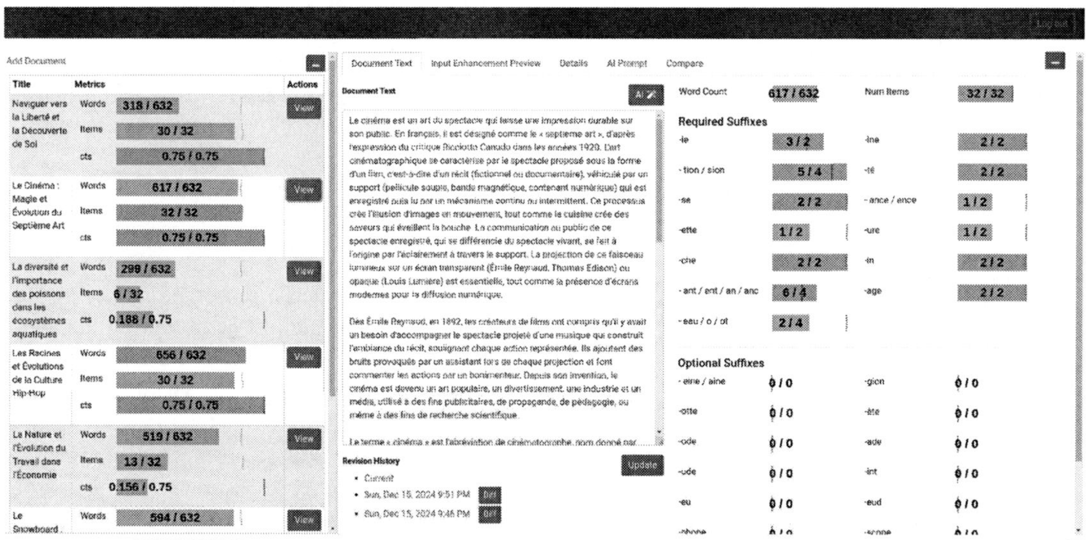

Figure 3: The tool interface allows authors to quickly scan the "readiness" of each document in the author's collection (left, see Section 4). Detailed metrics about specific linguistic shortcomings for a document are also available (right). To address the shortcomings, authors can click on the "AI" button to automatically generate a prompt that instructs an LLM to make specific edits to the document, which is then sent to a remote LLM service. The modified text is saved as a new version, and "Input Enhancement" and "Compare" views are available to help the author quickly see how the text has been edited.

Two other views that support the author worth briefly mentioning are 1) a Diff Viewer component (Ravi, 2024) that allows comparison of the old and new versions for authors to quickly review changes after an iteration of LLM edits, and 2) an Input Enhancement view that highlights target forms to allow the author to quickly locate them in the text.

5 Plans for evaluation

Evaluating the proposed LLM-based method and the authoring tool is an important step that we are currently planning. For the first evaluation we plan on using human judgements by French native speakers to evaluate a set of modified documents. The five measures used by Shu et al. (2024) in their evaluation of LLM performance on rewriting tasks seem to capture all the dimensions of the text quality we would be concerned with:

1. **Instruction success**: whether the rewrite accurately follows the instruction provided.
2. **Content preservation**: whether the rewritten text preserves the essential content and meaning of the source text, regardless of its writing style or quality.
3. **Factuality**: Checks the accuracy and truthfulness of the answer's content.
4. **Coherence**: whether the rewritten text is easy to understand, non-ambiguous, and logically coherent when read by itself (without checking against the source text).
5. **Fluency**: Examines the clarity, grammar, and style of the written answer.

(Shu et al., 2024, p. 18974)

Since the tool's main purpose is to introduce new target linguistic structures into an existing text, it will be important to check whether or not the LLM model actually inserts strings featuring the needed target forms without modifying them (an LLM may try to modify the strings so that they fit better in the text but no longer count as a valid instance of a target linguistic structure).

Of course, ensuring that the strings are present in the text is not, by itself, a good reflection of how well the edits were performed. The whole point of the method is to try to carry out the edit instructions while preserving the original meaning of the text, so that it can continue to serve as a meaningful context for instruction (see Section 2.1). The dimensions of *content preservation* ("Have the messages conveyed by the text changed?") and *coherence* ("Is the text as easy to understand and as logically coherent as it was before the edits?") are therefore important performance criteria for ensuring that the text remains a valid meaningful context.

Since the texts will serve language learners as models of well-formed L2 writing, another important dimension of performance is how linguistically correct the edits are. Shu et al. (2024) use the label 'fluency', which in SLA literature is used to refer to how well language flows (e.g. Housen and Kuiken, 2009), but in our case it seems more important to measure the linguistic correctness, or accuracy, of the modified texts, to investigate if LLMs introduce grammatically incorrect language into their output.

Regarding *factuality*, it is well-known that LLMs can hallucinate, i.e., generate text that includes untrue or misleading information (Huang et al., 2024). Of course, an authentic text could already contain factually untrue information, but the point of including this measure would be to understand whether or not new factually incorrect information is introduced during the editing task.

6 Conclusion

In this paper we presented a new authoring tool aimed at solving a practical issue with using authentic texts to contextualise grammar practice, namely that authentic texts usually do not contain a sufficient number or variety of linguistic structures needed to support L2 input and output practice exercises with a specific grammar target. The tool relies on a method that proposes combining traditional natural language generation, using lexical databases and rule-based tools, with current LLM services to dynamically generate prompts that instruct an LLM to insert strings with specific linguistic structures into the text.

Our experience with the tool so far is encouraging, but to really determine the viability of the approach a formal evaluation is needed. The next step will be to carry out a first evaluation with human judgements using the criteria presented in Section 5, possibly while also exploring the impact of different prompt formulations, and different LLM service providers and models.

Assuming that the method is successful, two other issues may arise. A first issue has to do with the current high computational cost of using LLMs: the best performing LLMs cannot be self-hosted due to their high computational cost which means that our tool currently depends on paid

LLM service providers. This places a limit on how many documents an organisation can rewrite before hitting budget limits. A second issue has to do with copyrighted materials. While authentic texts that are in public domain or released with permissive licenses allowing derivatives shouldn't be an issue, it seems likely that many useful texts will be copyrighted; even if use for educational purposes is permitted, rewriting the material seems to go one step further and could be problematic. These are issues that need further consideration.

References

Itziar Aldabe, Maddalen Lopez de Lacalle, Montse Maritxalar, Edurne Martinez, and Larraitz Uria. 2006. ArikIturri: An Automatic Question Generator Based on Corpora and NLP Techniques. In *Intelligent Tutoring Systems*, volume 4053 of *Lecture Notes in Computer Science*, pages 584–594. Springer.

L. Antonsen and C. Argese. 2018. Using authentic texts for grammar exercises for a minority language. In *Linköping Electronic Conference Proceedings*, page 152.

J. Baptista, S. Lourenco, and N. J. Mamede. 2016. Automatic generation of exercises on passive transformation in Portuguese. In *2016 IEEE Congress on Evolutionary Computation (CEC)*, pages 4965–4972.

Jean-Pierre Berwald. 1987. *Teaching Foreign Languages with Realia and Other Authentic Materials. ERIC Q&A*. Distributed by ERIC Clearinghouse, S.l. Sponsoring Agency: Office of Educational Research and Improvement (ED), Washington, DC.

Stephen Bodnar. 2022. The instructional effectiveness of automatically generated exercises for learning French grammatical gender: preliminary results. In *Proceedings of the 11th Workshop on NLP for Computer Assisted Language Learning*, pages 10–22, Louvain-la-Neuve, Belgium. LiU Electronic Press.

Jill Burstein, Nitin Madnani, John Sabatini, Dan McCaffrey, Kietha Biggers, and Kelsey Dreier. 2017. Generating language activities in real-time for english learners using language muse. In *Proceedings of the Fourth ACM Conference on Learning @ Scale, L@S 2017, Cambridge, MA, USA, April 20-21, 2017*, pages 213–215. ACM.

Antoine Chalvin, Egle Eensoo, and François Stuck. 2013. Mining a parallel corpus for automatic generation of Estonian grammar exercises. In *Third biennial conference on electronic lexicography (eLex 2013) "Electronic lexicography in the 21st century: thinking outside the paper"*, pages 280–295, Tallinn, Estonia.

Sophia Chan, Swapna Somasundaran, Debanjan Ghosh, and Mengxuan Zhao. 2022. AGReE: A system for generating automated grammar reading exercises. In *Proceedings of the 2022 Conference on Empirical Methods in Natural Language Processing: System Demonstrations*, pages 169–177, Abu Dhabi, UAE. Association for Computational Linguistics.

Maria Chinkina and Detmar Meurers. 2016. Linguistically aware information retrieval: Providing input enrichment for second language learners. In *Proceedings of the 11th Workshop on Innovative Use of NLP for Building Educational Applications*, pages 188–198, San Diego, CA. Association for Computational Linguistics.

Leona Colling, Ines Pieronczyk, Cora Parrisius, Heiko Holz, Stephen Bodnar, Florian Nuxoll, and Detmar Meurers. 2024. Towards task-oriented icall: A criterion-referenced learner dashboard organising digital practice. In *Proceedings of the 16th International Conference on Computer Supported Education - Volume 1: EKM*, pages 668–679. INSTICC, SciTePress.

Frederik Cornillie, Ruben Lagatie, Mieke Vandewaetere, Geraldine Clarebout, and Piet Desmet. 2013. Tools that detectives use: In search of learner-related determinants for usage of optional feedback in a written murder mystery. *CALICO Journal*, 30:22–45.

Sabrina Dittrich, Zarah Weiss, Hannes Schröter, and Detmar Meurers. 2019. Integrating large-scale web data and curated corpus data in a search engine supporting German literacy education. In *Proceedings of the 8th Workshop on NLP for Computer Assisted Language Learning*, pages 41–56, Turku, Finland. LiU Electronic Press.

Zoltán Dörnyei and Ema Ushioda. 2011. *Teaching and researching motivation (2nd ed.)*. Harlow: Longman.

Polina Drozdova, Catia Cucchiarini, and Helmer Strik. 2013. L2 syntax acquisition: the effect of oral and written computer assisted practice. In *14th Annual Conference of the International Speech Communication Association, INTERSPEECH 2013, Lyon, France, August 25-29, 2013*, pages 982–986. ISCA.

Albert Gatt and Ehud Reiter. 2009. Simplenlg: a realisation engine for practical applications. In *Proceedings of the 12th European Workshop on Natural Language Generation*, ENLG '09, page 90–93, USA. Association for Computational Linguistics.

Alex Gilmore. 2007. Authentic materials and authenticity in foreign language learning. *Language Teaching*, 40(2):97–118.

Masato Hagiwara, Joshua Tanner, and Keisuke Sakaguchi. 2021. Grammartagger: A multilingual, minimally-supervised grammar profiler for language education.

Tanja Heck and Detmar Meurers. 2022. Parametrizable exercise generation from authentic texts: Effectively targeting the language means on the curriculum. In *Proceedings of the 17th Workshop on Innovative Use of NLP for Building Educational Applications (BEA 2022)*, pages 154–166, Seattle, Washington. Association for Computational Linguistics.

A. Housen and F. Kuiken. 2009. Complexity, accuracy, and fluency in second language acquisition. *Applied Linguistics*, 30(4):461–473.

Lei Huang, Weijiang Yu, Weitao Ma, Weihong Zhong, Zhangyin Feng, Haotian Wang, Qianglong Chen, Weihua Peng, Xiaocheng Feng, Bing Qin, and Ting Liu. 2024. A survey on hallucination in large language models: Principles, taxonomy, challenges, and open questions. *ACM Trans. Inf. Syst.* Just Accepted.

Gladys Jean and Daphnée Simard. 2011. Grammar teaching and learning in l2: Necessary, but boring? *Foreign Language Annals*, 44(3):467–494.

R. Lyster. 2018. *Content-based Language Teaching*. New York: Routledge.

Roy Lyster. 2006. Predictability in french gender attribution: A corpus analysis. *Journal of French Language Studies*, 16(1):69–92.

Christopher D. Manning, Mihai Surdeanu, John Bauer, Jenny Finkel, Steven J. Bethard, and David McClosky. 2014. The Stanford CoreNLP natural language processing toolkit. In *Association for Computational Linguistics (ACL) System Demonstrations*, pages 55–60.

Detmar Meurers, Ramon Ziai, Luiz Amaral, Adriane Boyd, Aleksandar Dimitrov, Vanessa Metcalf, and Niels Ott. 2010. Enhancing authentic web pages for language learners. In *Proceedings of the NAACL HLT 2010 Fifth Workshop on Innovative Use of NLP for Building Educational Applications*, pages 10–18, Los Angeles, California. Association for Computational Linguistics.

Boris New, Christophe Pallier, and Ludovic Brysbaert, Marc andFerrand. 2004. Lexique 2 : A new French lexical database. *Behavior Research Methods, Instruments, &amp Computers*, 36(3):516–524.

Laura Perez-Beltrachini, Claire Gardent, and German Kruszewski. 2012. Generating Grammar Exercises. In *NAACL-HLT 7th Workshop on Innovative Use of NLP for Building Educational Applications*, Montreal, Canada.

Pranesh Ravi. 2024. https://praneshravi.in/react-diff-viewer/. Accessed on December 16th, 2024. [link].

Robert Reynolds, Eduard Schaf, and Detmar Meurers. 2014. A VIEW of Russian: Visual input enhancement and adaptive feedback. In *Proceedings of the third workshop on NLP for computer-assisted language learning*, pages 98–112, Uppsala, Sweden. LiU Electronic Press.

Lei Shu, Liangchen Luo, Jayakumar Hoskere, Yun Zhu, Yinxiao Liu, Simon Tong, Jindong Chen, and Lei Meng. 2024. Rewritelm: An instruction-tuned large language model for text rewriting. *Proceedings of the AAAI Conference on Artificial Intelligence*, 38(17):18970–18980.

SimpleNLG. https://github.com/simplenlg/simplenlg. Accessed on December 15th, 2024. [link].

Helmer Strik, Polina Drozdova, and Catia Cucchiarini. 2013. Gobl: Games online for basic language learning. In *Speech and Language Technology in Education (SLaTE 2013)*, pages 137–142.

Jingfeng Yang, Hongye Jin, Ruixiang Tang, Xiaotian Han, Qizhang Feng, Haoming Jiang, Shaochen Zhong, Bing Yin, and Xia Hu. 2024. Harnessing the power of llms in practice: A survey on chatgpt and beyond. *ACM Trans. Knowl. Discov. Data*, 18(6).

Ines Zelch, Matthias Hagen, and Martin Potthast. 2024. A user study on the acceptance of native advertising in generative ir. In *Proceedings of the 2024 Conference on Human Information Interaction and Retrieval*, CHIIR '24, page 142–152, New York, NY, USA. Association for Computing Machinery.

Nicole Ziegler, Detmar Meurers, Patrick Rebuschat, Simón Ruiz, José L. Moreno-Vega, Maria Chinkina, Wenjing Li, and Sarah Grey. 2017. Interdisciplinary research at the intersection of call, nlp, and sla: Methodological implications from an input enhancement project. *Language Learning*, 67(S1):209–231.

PIRLS Category-specific Question Generation for Reading Comprehension

Yin Poon[1], **Qiong Wang**[2], **John S. Y. Lee**[2], **Yu Yan Lam**[1], **Samuel Kai Wah Chu**[1]

[1]School of Nursing and Health Studies, Hong Kong Metropolitan University,
{ypoon, yuylam, skwchu}@hkmu.edu.hk
[2]Department of Linguistics and Translation, City University of Hong Kong,
{wang.qiong, jsylee}@cityu.edu.hk

Abstract

According to the internationally recognized PIRLS (Progress in International Reading Literacy Study) assessment standards, reading comprehension questions should encompass all four comprehension processes: retrieval, inferencing, integrating and evaluation. This paper investigates whether Large Language Models can produce high-quality questions for each of these categories. Human assessment on a Chinese dataset shows that GPT-4o can generate usable and category-specific questions, ranging from 74% to 90% accuracy depending on the category.

1 Introduction

Given the importance of asking questions for effective learning (Dillon, 2006; Etemadzadeh et al., 2013; Kurdi et al., 2020), there has been extensive effort in developing automatic Question Generation (QG) models to produce high-quality questions for reading materials in educational systems (Heilman and Smith, 2010; Lindberg et al., 2013). Through automatic creation of pedagogical and assessment material, QG benefits teachers by reducing their workload. It also levels the playing field for students, providing them with instant and free access to questions for review and practice.

According to PIRLS (Progress in International Reading Literacy Study), reading requires four comprehension processes: retrieval, inferencing, integrating and evaluation (Mullis and Martin, 2019) as described in Table 1. A balanced set of questions, involving all four processes, is therefore needed to assess reading comprehension. However, existing QG benchmarks such as SQuAD (Rajpurkar et al., 2016) mostly focus on factoid short-answer questions.

Process	Description
Retrieval	Focus on and Retrieve Explicitly Stated Information
Inferencing	Make Straightforward Inferences
Integrating	Interpret and Integrate Ideas and Information
Evaluation	Evaluate and Critique Content and Textual Elements

Table 1: Comprehension processes in reading according to PIRLS (Mullis and Martin, 2019)

This paper investigates question generation of the four PIRLS categories with Large Language Models (LLMs) using zero-shot, few-shot and fine-tuning approaches. Our contribution is two-fold. In this first attempt of QG based on PIRLS, an internationally recognized standard for reading comprehension assessment, we show that GPT-4o can generate high-quality questions with category-specific prompts. Second, we contribute a dataset of Chinese passages and questions, annotated with PIRLS categories, as a benchmark for future research.[1]

2 Previous work

Early QG approaches mostly relied on heuristics, linguistic templates and rules (Labutov et al., 2015; Mostow et al., 2016). With the availability of large-scale datasets, QG began to be formulated as a sequence-to-sequence generation task. An encoder-decoder architecture with a global attention mechanism was found to be effective (Du et al., 2017; Kim et al., 2019), but can be further improved with transformer-based approaches (Scialom et al., 2019), and fully fine-tuned language models (LM) (Xiao et al., 2021). Answer-agnostic QG can be performed via joint Question and Answer Generation (QAG) (Lewis et al., 2021). A QAG model based on fine-tuning

[1]Code and data for this paper are available at `https://github.com/pypoon/PIRLS-QG-ZH`

Yin Poon, Qiong Wang, John S. Y. Lee, Yu Yan Lam and Samuel Kai Wah Chu. PIRLS Category-specific Question Generation for Reading Comprehension. *Proceedings of the 14th Workshop on Natural Language Processing for Computer Assisted Language Learning (NLP4CALL 2025)*. University of Tartu Library. 72–80.

Excerpt of input passage (in Chinese):	
传统的「英式奶茶」采用名贵锡兰红茶，加入牛奶和糖冲泡，饮用时会配以蛋糕。...「港式奶茶」的对象是一般市民，食肆会选用较廉价的茶叶和淡奶，以降低成本。...此外，为配合华人喜欢喝浓茶的习惯，「港式奶茶」茶味普遍较浓。... The traditional "British milk tea" is made from posh Ceylon black tea, added with milk and sugar, and served with cake. ... "Hong Kong-style milk tea" is aimed at the general public, and restaurants will use cheaper tea leaves and evaporated milk to reduce costs. ... In addition, to match the Chinese habit of drinking strong tea, "Hong Kong-style milk tea" generally has a stronger tea flavor. ...	
Type	**Example Question**
Retrieval	食肆如何降低奶茶的制作成本？ How can restaurants reduce the cost of making milk tea?
Inferencing	「英式奶茶」的目标客户群是哪些人？ Who are the target customers of "British milk tea"?
Integrating	「英式奶茶」和「港式奶茶」有什么区别？ What is the difference between "British milk tea" and "Hong Kong-style milk" tea?
Evaluation	作者先介绍「英式奶茶」,再介绍「港式奶茶」。作者为什么这样安排？ The author first introduces "British milk tea" and then "Hong Kong-style milk tea". Why did the author arrange it this way?

Table 2: Example input passage and output questions of each PIRLS question type (Section 4)

encoder-decoder LMs produces high-quality questions (Ushio et al., 2022), but has not been evaluated in terms of question type. The most recent research has adopted LLMs. On a textbook dataset, few-shot prompting with GPT-3 was able to generate human-like questions ready for classroom use (Wang et al., 2022). A fine-tuned version of ChatGPT was able to generate questions that are competitive with human ones (Xiao et al., 2023).

Type-specific QG enables the user to request questions that suit their purposes. Controllable question generation has mainly focused on difficulty (Uto et al., 2023) and content (Li and Zhang, 2024), such as action, feeling, or setting. While Cao and Wang (2021) attempted QG according to a question topology (Olney et al., 2012), their approach was primarily template-based. In a study most closely related to ours, Elkins et al. (2023) used InstructGPT to generate six kinds of questions in Bloom's taxonomy (Krathwohl, 2002). Experimental results on Wikipedia passages on various disciplines showed that accuracy varied widely, from 36.1% to 91.7% across different categories. Since neither Olney's or Bloom's Taxonomy is designed for grade-school reading comprehension, this project will adopt the PIRLS framework. Further, we report the effect of fine-tuning LLMs and contribute a dataset in Chinese, which has more limited resources for QG.

3 Dataset

Existing reading comprehension datasets in Chinese, such as the Delta Reading Comprehension Dataset[2] and DuReader[3], are primarily drawn from newspapers, Wikipedia and user logs. Further, the questions are not annotated with their categories. We therefore constructed new datasets using Chinese-language pedagogical materials:

Training set The fine-tuning data consists of 804 manually composed questions about 72 passages taken from published Chinese story books. The average passage length is 1,131 Chinese characters. There are a total of 201 questions for each PIRLS category; 181 questions of these were used for training, and the remaining 20 for validation.

Test set The test set consists of 50 passages from a public reading comprehension assessment[4], with 25 passages from Grade 3, and 25 passages from Grade 6. The average passage length is 648 Chinese characters.

[2]https://github.com/DRCKnowledgeTeam/DRCD

[3]https://github.com/baidu/DuReader

[4]Downloaded from the website of the Territory-wide System Assessment (TSA) `https://www.bca.hkeaa.edu.hk/web/TSA/en/PriPaperSchema.html`.

4 Annotation Scheme

According to the International Association for the Evaluation of Educational Achievement, a reading comprehension question should address the following comprehension processes, as defined in the PIRLS standards (Table 1):

Retrieval The answer is explicitly given in a text span in the passage.

Inferencing Answering the question requires inferences about ideas or information that is not explicitly stated.

Integrating Answering the question "requires comprehension of the entire text, or at least significant portions of it." (Mullis and Martin, 2019)

Evaluation The answer "involves a judgement about some aspect of the text", and is not necessarily found in the passage.

Example questions for each category can be found in Table 2.[5]

5 Approach

The input is a Chinese text, without any specified answer span. We used two LLMs — GPT-4o[6] and *LLaMa-3* (Cui and Yao, 2024)[7] to generate questions[8] for the text, using the following prompts (see prompts in Table 6):

Zero-shot For each of the four PIRLS category, a different prompt describing the requirements of the category is used.

Generic Unlike the zero-shot approach, the prompt does not specify the question category. This serves to gauge the effectiveness of the description of PIRLS categories used in the zero-shot prompt.

Few-shot The PIRLS category-specific prompt used in zero-shot above is accompanied with an input passage and N sample questions, according to the template in Table 8 (Appendix B). We set $N = 5$, with a sample passage and five questions taken from the training set.

Fine-tuned We fine-tuned[9] LLaMa-3 on the training set (Section 3), using the PIRLS category-specific prompts shown in Table 6.

For each passage in the test set, a question was generated from each prompt type described above.

Model	Unusable	Usable	
		minor rev.	wo/ rev.
Llama-3 (generic)	4%	24%	72%
Llama-3 (zero-shot)	4%	17.5%	78.5%
Llama-3 (few-shot)	14%	15%	71%
Llama-3 (fine-tuned)	15%	26.5%	58.5%
GPT-4o (generic)	2%	10%	88%
GPT-4o (zero-shot)	**0%**	**4%**	**96%**

Table 3: Evaluation results on usability using the scale defined in Section 6

6 Evaluation set-up

Four assessors, all native Chinese speakers with a bachelor's degree, annotated each generated question on its *usability* and *PIRLS category*. The order of the questions was randomized to avoid bias. Each question was independently evaluated by two of the assessors. In case of disagreement, a PIRLS expert with a Master's degree in Education, adjudicated the decision.

First, the assessors rated the quality of the question on the following three-point scale:

Usable without revision The question can be used as is: it is grammatical, fluent, and relevant for the input passage.

Usable with minor revision The question is relevant for the input passage, but requires improvement in its linguistic quality, e.g., correction of grammatical errors, better vocabulary choice or phrasing.

Unusable The question is irrelevant for the passage, or cannot be understood.

[5] The Chinese passage is taken from a Chinese-language public examination at https://www.hkeaa.edu.hk/en/sa_tsa/

[6] https://openai.com/index/hello-gpt-4o/

[7] Chinese 8B Instruct-v1, downloaded from https://huggingface.co/hfl/llama-3-chinese-8b-instruct

[8] max_tokens=200; temperature=0.6; top_p=0.9 for both LLMs

[9] The fine-tuning was performed for 1 epoch using the following hyperparameters: learning rate=1e-4; lora_rank=64; lora_alpha=128; lora_dropout=0.05; batch_size = 1; gradient_accumulation_steps=8; max_seq_length=3303. On an A100 GPU, the training took 4 minutes and 34 seconds.

Model	PIRLS category				Average
	Retrieval	Inferencing	Integrating	Evaluation	
Llama-3 (generic)	56%	32%	8%	0%	24%
Llama-3 (zero-shot)	78%	40%	22%	20%	40%
Llama-3 (few-shot)	82%	26%	10%	4%	30.5%
Llama-3 (fine-tuned)	68%	42%	10%	34%	38.5%
GPT-4o (generic)	54%	32%	12%	0%	24.5%
GPT-4o (zero-shot)	**86%**	**74%**	**78%**	**90%**	82%

Table 4: Accuracy in question category (denominator includes unusable questions)

Category	Retrieval	Infer.	Integr.	Eval.
Retrieval	**43**	6	1	0
Infer.	8	**37**	3	2
Integr.	0	3	**39**	8
Eval.	0	0	5	**45**

Table 5: Confusion matrix of the PIRLS category of the questions generated by GPT-4o (zero-shot)

Then, the usable questions (either without revision or with minor revision) were classified in terms of PIRLS question type (Section 4).

7 Results

7.1 Question Usability

Inter-annotator agreement. The four assessors agreed on 90% of questions on the usable vs. unusable classification, leading to a 0.499 weighted Kappa score, a "moderate" level of agreement (Landis and Koch, 1977).

Usability. Using the generic prompt, only 72% of the questions generated by Llama-3 were usable without revision (Table 3). The category-specific zero-shot prompt, which supplied more detailed requirements on the questions to be generated, increased the proportion of directly usable questions to 78.5%. Providing examples through few-shot and fine-tuning, however, resulted in more unusable questions. Our human evaluators reported that the model was led to overly prefer the wording in the given samples, even if it results in unnatural questions.

On GPT-4o, the category-specific prompts also led to gains in usability over the generic one. Overall, GPT-4o attained substantially superior performance, with a vast majority of the generated questions (96%) assessed as directly usable.

7.2 Question category

Inter-annotator agreement. Excluding the unusable questions, the assessors agreed on 55.17% of the generated questions on the 4-way classification of PIRLS category. This yielded a 0.494 weighted kappa score, a "moderate" level of agreement (Landis and Koch, 1977).

Accuracy in category. As expected, the generic prompt, which gave no specific instruction on question category, led to the lowest accuracy for both Llama-3 (24%) and GPT-4o (24.5%). Both models would be hardly useful for teachers looking for higher-order questions that require inferencing, integrating or evaluation, since they produced mostly 'retrieval'-type questions (56% and 54%, respectively). The category-specific (zero-shot) prompts improved the accuracy across all categories, raising the average accuracy to 40% for Llama-3 and 82% for GPT-4o. This result suggests that both models were able to understand the instructions in the prompt.

On Llama-3, the few-shot approach improved the generation of 'retrieval' questions to 82%. The five samples, however, appeared to be insufficient for the higher-order categories, resulting in lower accuracy. With larger quantity of training data for these higher-order categories, the fine-tuned model offered better performance for 'Inferencing' and 'Evaluation'.

The GPT-4o zero-shot approach achieved the best performance across all categories, with an average of 82% accuracy. As shown in the confusion matrix (Table 5), most errors were within one category above or below the target in the PIRLS scale.

8 Conclusion

A variety of question types, targeting various comprehension processes, is necessary for assessing reading comprehension. This paper has presented the first study on automatic question generation for reading comprehension based on the four categories in the PIRLS framework. Experiments on

Chinese passages show that zero-shot GPT-4o can produce questions belonging to the target category at 74% to 90% accuracy, outperforming both the zero-shot and fine-tuned LLaMA-3 model.

This research has focused on assisting teachers in designing a variety of question types, to test students' skills in reading comprehension. In future work, we plan to extend the experiment to the quality of the answers, to further automate the test design process. We also plan to deploy the automatically generated questions in real-world classrooms to measure their pedagogical impact on students.

Limitations and Ethics Consideration

At the time of system deployment, users should be clearly informed that the automatically generated questions should be viewed only as a first draft, to minimize the risk that the teacher may fail to edit an unusable question and pass it to students.

Considering the high cost of using few-shot generation, we did not test GPT-4o on few-shot prompts in this paper. Typically, generating integrating and evaluation questions requires a full text or several passages. Our focus was on finding a cost-effective approach to generate reading comprehension questions. Therefore, we suggest that future research explore the few-shot prompts in GPT-4o.

Acknowledgements

We gratefully acknowledge support from the e-Learning Ancillary Facilities Programme of the Quality Education Fund (Project "Knowledge Overlord - A Self-sustaining AI Game-based Online Platform to Enhance Student's Literacy Ability and 21st Century Skills"); and from a Teaching Development Grant at City University of Hong Kong (project 6000834).

References

Shuyang Cao and Lu Wang. 2021. Controllable Open-ended Question Generation with A New Question Type Ontology. In *Proc. 59th Annual Meeting of the Association for Computational Linguistics*, page 6424–6439.

Y. Cui and X. Yao. 2024. Rethinking LLM Language Adaptation: A Case Study on Chinese Mixtral. In *arXiv preprint arXiv:2403.01851*.

James T. Dillon. 2006. Effect of questions in education and other enterprises. In *Rethinking schooling*, page 145–174. Routledge.

Xinya Du, Junru Shao, and Claire Cardie. 2017. Learning to Ask: Neural Question Generation for Reading Comprehension. In *Proceedings of the 55th Annual Meeting of the Association for Computational Linguistics (ACL)*.

Sabina Elkins, Ekaterina Kochmar, Iulian Serban, and Jackie C. K. Cheung. 2023. How Useful Are Educational Questions Generated by Large Language Models? *AIED 2023, CCIS*, 1831:536–542.

Atika Etemadzadeh, Samira Seifi, and Hamid Roohbakhsh Far. 2013. The role of questioning technique in developing thinking skills: The ongoing effect on writing skill. *Procedia-Social and Behavioral Sciences*, 70:1024–1031.

Michael Heilman and Noah A. Smith. 2010. Good Question! Statistical Ranking for Question Generation. In *Proc. Human Language Technologies: The 2010 Annual Conference of the North American Chapter of the ACL (HLT-NAACL)*, page 609–617.

Yanghoon Kim, Hwanhee Lee, Joongbo Shin, and Kyomin Jung. 2019. Improving Neural Question Generation Using Answer Separation. In *Proc. 33rd AAAI Conference on Artificial Intelligence (AAAI-19)*.

D. R. Krathwohl. 2002. A revision of Bloom's taxonomy: An overview. *Theory into practice*, 41(4):212–218.

Ghader Kurdi, Jared Leo, Bijan Parsia, Uli Sattler, and Salam Al-Emari. 2020. A systematic review of automatic question generation for educational purposes. *International Journal of Artificial Intelligence in Education*, 30:121–204.

I. Labutov, S. Basu, and L. Vanderwende. 2015. Deep questions without deep understanding. In *Proc. ACL*.

J. Richard Landis and Gary G. Koch. 1977. The Measurement of Observer Agreement for Categorical Data. *Biometrics*, 33:159–174.

Patrick Lewis, Yuxiang Wu, Linqing Liu, Pasquale Minervini, Heinrich Küttler, Aleksandra Piktus, Pontus Stenetorp, and Sebastian Riedel. 2021. PAQ: 65 million probably-asked questions and what you can do with them. *Transactions of the Association for Computational Linguistics*, 9:1098–1115.

Kunze Li and Yu Zhang. 2024. Planning first, question second: An llm-guided method for controllable question generation. In *indings of the Association for Computational Linguistics ACL 2024*, page 4715–4729.

David Lindberg, Fred Popowich, John Nesbit, and Phil Winne. 2013. Generating natural language questions to support learning on-line. In *Proceedings of the 14th European Workshop on Natural Language Generation*, page 105–114.

Jack Mostow, Yi ting Huang, Hyeju Jang, Anders Weinstein, Joe Valeri, and Donna Gates. 2016. Developing, evaluating, and refining an automatic generator of diagnostic multiple choice cloze questions to assess children's comprehension while reading. *Natural Language Engineering*, 23(2):245–294.

Ina V. S. Mullis and Michael O. Martin. 2019. *PIRLS 2021 Assessment Frameworks*. International Association for the Evaluation of Educational Achievement.

Andrew M. Olney, Arthur C. Graesser, and Natalie K. Person. 2012. Question generation from concept maps. *Dialogue and Discourse*, 3(2):75–99.

Pranav Rajpurkar, Jian Zhang, Konstantin Lopyrev, and Percy Liang. 2016. SQuAD: 100,000+ Questions for Machine Comprehension of Text. In *Proc. Conference on Empirical Methods in Natural Language Processing (EMNLP)*, page 2383–2392.

Thomas Scialom, Benjamin Piwowarski, and Jacopo Staiano. 2019. Self-Attention Architectures for Answer-Agnostic Neural Question Generation. In *Proceedings of the 57th Annual Meeting of the Association for Computational Linguistics*, page 6027–6032.

Asahi Ushio, Fernando Alva-Manchego, and Jose Camacho-Collados. 2022. Generative Language Models for Paragraph-Level Question Generation. In *Proceedings of the 2022 Conference on Empirical Methods in Natural Language Processing*, page 670–688.

Masaki Uto, Yuto Tomikawa, and Ayaka Suzuki. 2023. Difficulty-Controllable Neural Question Generation for Reading Comprehension using Item Response Theory. In *Proc. 18th Workshop on Innovative Use of NLP for Building Educational Applications (BEA 2023)*, page 119–129.

Z. Wang, J. Valdez, D. Basu Mallick, and R. G. Baraniuk. 2022. Towards Human-Like Educational Question Generation with Large Language Models. *Artificial Intelligence in Education. AIED 2022. Lecture Notes in Computer Science*, 13355.

Changrong Xiao, Sean Xin Xu, Kunpeng Zhang, Yufang Wang, and Lei Xia. 2023. Evaluating reading comprehension exercises generated by llms: A showcase of chatgpt in education applications. In *Proc. 18th Workshop on Innovative Use of NLP for Building Educational Applications*, page 610–625.

Dongling Xiao, Han Zhang, Yukun Li, Yu Sun, Hao Tian, Hua Wu, and Haifeng Wang. 2021. Ernie-gen: an enhanced multi-flow pre-training and fine-tuning framework for natural language generation. In *Proceedings of the Twenty-Ninth International Conference on International Joint Conferences on Artificial Intelligence*, page 3997–4003.

A Appendix: Instruction to Human Assessors

The human assessors gave consent to the data collection and were informed that the results would remain anonymous. They were shown the following instructions:

```
<passage>
<question>
```

1. Is the question understandable and relevant for the passage?
2. Does the language quality of the question need to be improved?
3. If the answer to #1 is "Yes", choose one of the categories for the question:
   - Retrieval (Focus on and Retrieve Explicitly Stated Information)
   - Inferencing (Make Straightforward Inferences)
   - Integrating (Interpret and Integrate Ideas and Information)
   - Evaluation (Evaluate and Critique Content Textual Elements)

B Appendix: Few-shot prompt template

The prompts are shown in Table 6, and their English translation in Table 7. The few-shot template is shown in Table 8.

Type	Prompt (in Chinese)
System prompt	你是一個能幹的閱讀理解問題生成器，始終遵循給定的說明和要求來生成問題。
Generic prompt	基於所提供的文章，請創作一個簡答題，並提供對應的答案。 文章:{input passage}
Retrieval questions (PIRLS level 1)	基於所提供的文章，請創作一個屬於PIRLS第一層次的簡答題， 並提供對應的答案。這個問題應著重於檢索文本中明確表述的信息，也就是資訊檢索型的問題。此類問題要求考生識別和回憶文本中明確提到的信息，如事件的順序、角色的特徵或進行比較等。 文章:{input passage}
Inferencing questions (PIRLS level 2)	基於所提供的文章，請創作一個屬於PIRLS第二層次的簡答題， 並提供對應的答案。這個問題應鼓勵考生從文本中進行直接推理，進一步超越單純的信息提取，也就是需要進行簡單推理的問題。 這類問題需要考生進行直接推理，例如理解因果關係或推測未明確陳述但可以從文本邏輯推導出的結果。 文章:{input passage}
Integrating questions (PIRLS level 3)	基於所提供的文章，請創作一個屬於PIRLS第三層次的簡答題， 並提供對應的答案。這個問題應促使考生解釋想法並整合文本不同部分信息，也就是需要進行解釋及整合的問題。這類問題需要考生全面理解並能夠從文本的不同部分綜合信息，如解釋角色的感受和行為，並整合文本中的想法和信息。 文章:{input passage}
Evaluation questions (PIRLS level 4)	基於所提供的文章，請創作一個屬於PIRLS第四層次的簡答題， 並提供對應的答案。這個問題應需要考生批判性地檢視和評估文本內容、語言和文本元素，也就是評鑒型的問題。這類問題是最高層次的問題，問題挑戰考生批判性地評估文本的內容、語言和文本元素，如對價值、期望和接受度作出判斷，或考慮他們如果處於某個角色的位置會如何反應。 文章:{input passage}

Table 6: LLM prompts for generating questions for each PIRLS category

Type	Prompt (in English)
System prompt	You are a capable reading comprehension question generator, always following the given instructions and requirements to generate questions.
Generic prompt	Based on the given passage, create a short-answer question and provide a corresponding answer. article:{input passage}
Retrieval questions (PIRLS level 1)	Based on the article provided, please create a short answer question belonging to PIRLS level 1 and provide the corresponding answer. This question should focus on retrieving information explicitly stated in the text, i.e. an information retrieval type question. This kind of question requires candidates to identify and recall information explicitly mentioned in the text, such as the sequence of events, character traits, or making comparisons. article:{input passage}
Inferencing questions (PIRLS level 2)	Based on the article provided, please create a short answer question belonging to PIRLS level 2 and provide the corresponding answer. This question should encourage candidates to make straightforward inferences from the article, moving further beyond information retrieval, i.e. a question requiring simple inferences. This type of question requires candidates to make straightforward inferences, such as understanding cause and effect relationships or inferring consequences that are not explicitly stated but can be logically deduced from the text. article:{input passage}
Integrating questions (PIRLS level 3)	Based on the article provided, please create a short answer question belonging to the PIRLS level 3 and provide the corresponding answer. This question should prompt the candidate to interpret ideas and integrate information from different parts of the text, i.e. a question that requires interpretation and integration. This type of question requires candidates to have a comprehensive understanding and be able to integrate information from different parts of the text, such as explaining a character's feelings and actions, and integrating ideas and information across the text. article:{input passage}
Evaluation questions (PIRLS level 4)	Based on the article provided, please create a short answer question belonging to PIRLS level 4 and provide the corresponding answer. This question should require candidates to critically examine and evaluate the text content, language, and textual elements, i.e. an evaluative question. This type of question is the highest-level question that challenges candidates to critically evaluate a text content, language, and textual elements, such as making judgments about value, desirability, and acceptability or considering how they would react if they were in a character's position. article:{input passage}

Table 7: LLM prompts for generating questions for each PIRLS category (English translation)

{category-specific prompt}
範例文章及相應的範例問題(請參考範例來創作問題):
{範例文章:{example passage}
PIRLS第{required level}層次範例問題1:{example question-answer pair 1}
...
PIRLS第{required level}層次範例問題5:{example question-answer pair 5}}
文章: {input passage}

Table 8: Prompt template for few-shot question generation

Investigating Linguistic Abilities of LLMs for Native Language Identification

Ahmet Yavuz Uluslu
University of Zurich
ahmetyavuz.uluslu@uzh.ch

Gerold Schneider
University of Zurich
gschneid@cl.uzh.ch

Abstract

Large language models (LLMs) have achieved state-of-the-art results in native language identification (NLI). However, these models often depend on superficial features, such as cultural references and self-disclosed information in the document, rather than capturing the underlying linguistic structures. In this work, we evaluate the linguistic abilities of open-source LLMs by evaluating their performance in NLI through content-independent features, such as POS n-grams, function words, and punctuation marks, and compare their performance against traditional machine learning approaches. Our experiments reveal that while LLM's initial performance on structural features (55.2% accuracy) falls significantly below their performance on full text (96.5%), fine-tuning significantly improves their capabilities, enabling state-of-the-art results with strong cross-domain generalization.

1 Introduction

Native Language Identification (NLI) aims to automatically determine an individual's native language (L1) based on their writing or speech in a second language (L2). This task is grounded in cross-linguistic influence theory, which posits that L1 leaves distinctive traces in the L2 production patterns (Yu and Odlin, 2016). NLI applications include providing metalinguistic feedback to language learners (Karim and Nassaji, 2020) and adapting grammatical error correction (GEC) systems based on L1 and proficiency level (Nadejde and Tetreault, 2020).

The top performing systems in the two previous shared tasks in NLI combined linguistic features with machine learning algorithms (Malmasi et al., 2017). Various feature types were investigated, including spelling errors, word and lemma n-grams, character n-grams, dependency trees, and morphosyntax (Markov et al., 2022). Recent advances in large language models (LLMs), particularly GPT-4 and LLaMA-3, demonstrate emergent metalinguistic abilities, including the capacity to process and analyze complex linguistic structures such as constituency trees of ambiguous sentences (Beguš et al., 2023). These newly acquired capabilities enabled the models to excel in downstream tasks such as NLI and GEC, which traditionally require thousands of examples to learn relatively complex linguistic relationships. Remarkably, LLMs achieve state-of-the-art performance in NLI on various benchmarks without any task-specific training (Zhang and Salle, 2023; Ng and Markov, 2024).

Despite their impressive performance, previous work has revealed that LLMs can rely on task-related shortcuts using superficial features, such as country names and cultural references, in the document rather than focusing on relevant linguistic features (Uluslu et al., 2024). Moreover, they often generate unfaithful explanations by failing to disclose their dependence on content-based hints in their reasoning process (Turpin et al., 2024). The close relationship between content and structural features makes it difficult to determine whether the models' success reflects their ability to perform genuine linguistic analysis or simply stems from pattern matching based on content cues.

The contributions of this work are the following: (i) we assess the linguistic abilities of open source LLMs through content-independent features, such as part-of-speech (POS) tags, function words, and punctuation marks, and compare their performance against traditional machine learning approaches, (ii) we demonstrate that while LLMs initially exhibit significant performance degradation when content words are replaced, indicating a strong dependence on lexical cues, fine-tuning

Ahmet Yavuz Uluslu and Gerold Schneider. Investigating Linguistic Abilities of LLMs for Native Language Identification. *Proceedings of the 14th Workshop on Natural Language Processing for Computer Assisted Language Learning (NLP4CALL 2025)*. University of Tartu Library. 81–88.

enables them to effectively leverage structural features, achieving state-of-the-art performance with robust cross-domain generalization.

2 Related Work

Linguistic probing Probing studies provide a systematic framework to analyze the linguistic knowledge encoded in LLM representations, demonstrating their ability to capture syntactic characteristics such as POS tags and dependency structures (Waldis et al., 2024). The approach employs a linear classifier trained on top of the model's contextual representations to predict specific linguistic properties. Following the key assumption of the probing paradigm, high classifier performance signals that model representations effectively encode the targeted linguistic phenomena (Belinkov, 2022).

Metalinguistic ability A crucial aspect of understanding language is metalinguistic ability, which refers to the ability to explicitly analyze and reason about linguistic structures and properties within a formal framework (Benelli et al., 2006). Although probing studies aim to reveal what linguistic information is encoded in model representations, they do not demonstrate the model's ability to perform explicit linguistic analysis. Moving beyond probing, Beguš et al. (2023) demonstrates that GPT-4 can generate formal syntactic tree analyses for ambiguous sentences, offering a more direct assessment of metalinguistic ability. Although the entanglement between linguistic performance and competence remains an open research question, recent discussions in the literature increasingly frame this analytical process as potential evidence of metalinguistic ability (Millière, 2024).

The impact on native language identification The emergence of metalinguistic performance in LLMs has significant implications for authorship analysis. Contemporary LLMs can explicitly analyze cross-linguistic influence, enabling them to identify word order influences and grammatical patterns that reveal an author's native language (Zhang and Salle, 2023). Earlier approaches using smaller models such as GPT-2 were based on learning probability distributions of various learner innovations specific to each L1 through the fine-tuning process (Uluslu and Schneider, 2022). The attempts to use a single GPT-2 model for the direct classification of L1 yielded suboptimal results. In these approaches, the surprisal of the model served as a proxy for L1 rather than an explicit analysis of the relevant linguistic features. Formally, for a text sequence $X = (x_1, ..., x_n)$, the surprisal S is defined as:

$$S(X) = -\sum_{i=1}^{n} \log P(x_i|x_{<i}) \quad (1)$$

To identify the native language L_1, separate language models M_{L_1} are trained for each potential linguistic background in $\mathcal{L}$. For a given text X, we compute surprisal scores using each language-specific model, and the final prediction is determined by identifying the model that yields the minimum surprisal:

$$L_1^* = \arg\min_{L_1 \in \mathcal{L}} S_{M_{L_1}}(X) \quad (2)$$

Although this approach showed strong results in the benchmarks, it suffered from poor cross-domain generalization (Vian, 2023), which we attribute to its strong lexical dependency, an inherent limitation of not being able to target specific linguistic features in the text. The most recent LLMs such as GPT-4 represent a fundamental shift in this regard, as they can explicitly identify and analyze task-relevant linguistic features out-of-the-box. This capability has been highlighted in previous studies, in which LLMs demonstrate state-of-the-art performance in zero-shot settings, eliminating the need for large training sets while simultaneously providing natural language explanations for their predictions (Zhang and Salle, 2023; Ng and Markov, 2024).

However, research indicates that such explanations, while superficially convincing, do not accurately represent the actual reasoning processes of the model (Turpin et al., 2024). Instead, the models frequently generate L1 predictions first and then construct plausible explanations, creating the illusion of metalinguistic analysis. This disconnect is problematic, as it allows findings to be selectively framed to support or refute any given authorship hypothesis (Ishihara et al., 2024). Evaluating linguistic abilities poses significant challenges in tasks like NLI, where distinguishing between cause and effect creates a chicken-and-egg problem: Does proficiency in grammatical error detection enable L1 identification, or does L1 identification reveal grammatical patterns? Although prompts can instruct models to attend to specific features, this constrained behavior still results in unfaithful explanations that often underestimate the influence of content-dependent features (Agarwal et al., 2024).

Content-independent features, widely adopted in authorship analysis research (Nini et al., 2024; Markov et al., 2022), offer a more robust approach by retaining structural patterns while minimizing the influence of topical and contextual cues. Markov et al. (2022) employs POS n-grams, function words, and punctuation marks with SVM, while Nini et al. (2024) constructs author-specific grammatical representations using n-gram models and compares disputed texts against these models using log-likelihood ratios. Both studies demonstrate that content-independent features can effectively capture structural patterns that generalize across domains. We investigate whether LLMs' claimed linguistic abilities reflect genuine analytical processes by examining their exploitation of structural features such as POS tags, function words, and punctuation patterns.

3 Dataset

The **TOEFL11** dataset (Blanchard, 2013) contains 1,100 essays in English, written by native speakers (L1) of 11 different languages. In total, there are 12,100 essays with an average of 348 tokens per essay. The essays were written in response to eight different writing topics, all of which appear in the 11 L1 groups, by authors with low, medium or high English proficiency. For our experiments, we focus on TOEFL4, a four-language subset of TOEFL11 (n=4400) that includes only essays written by native French, German, Italian, and Spanish speakers (Markov et al., 2022).

The **ICLE4-NLI** dataset, drawn from the ICLEv2 corpus (Granger et al., 2009), serves as our cross-domain evaluation benchmark. It contains 400 essays written by medium to high proficiency English learners, evenly distributed across four first languages of TOEFL4: French, German, Italian, and Spanish.

4 Methodology

To investigate the syntactic capabilities of LLMs, we adopted a methodology inspired by content-independent features of authorship analysis (Markov et al., 2022; Nini et al., 2024). Among various possible masking configurations shown in

Step	Sentence
Original	make products seem much better!
All POS	VB NNS VB RB JJ PUNCT
Ex. FW	make N seem much J PUNCT
Ex. FW-Punct	make N seem much J !

Table 1: The original sentence, its transformation into POS tags, POS tags except for function words, and the final form where both function words and punctuations are preserved.

Table 1, we use *Ex. FW-Punct* approach where each content word in the dataset is replaced (masked) with its corresponding POS tag, while retaining function words and punctuation marks to preserve structural patterns. The function words and phrases were identified using the POSNoise word list, which aims to mask topic-related words while preserving as much structural information as possible (Halvani and Graner, 2021). This approach allows certain delexicalised verbs, such as "make", to remain in their original form, compared to stop-word lists available in various open-source packages (Nothman et al., 2018).

4.1 Machine Learning with Linguistic Features

In our experiments, we use the liblinear implementation of support vector machines (SVM) from the scikit-learn library, using a one-vs-rest (OvR) strategy for multiclass classification (Pedregosa et al., 2011). To optimize hyperparameters, we perform a search over a range of regularization values $C \in 0.1, 1, 2.5, 5, 10$ and determine that the optimal value lies within the range of 2 to 2.5. Previous research has established the optimal POS n-gram range for this task as 1-3 (Malmasi and Dras, 2018). The experiments were evaluated using ten-fold cross-validation. This traditional machine learning baseline enables direct comparison of how effectively LLMs can exploit the same linguistic features.

4.2 LLM Analysis

For our experiments with LLMs, we employed LLaMA-3.1-8B-Instruct[1] and LLaMA-3.1-70B-Instruct to evaluate their zero-shot performance. The 70B model is particularly notable for being the most comparable to GPT-4 in NLI tasks under zero-shot settings (Uluslu et al., 2024). It was also

[1]https://huggingface.co/meta-llama/Llama-3.1-8B-Instruct

able to complete the previously mentioned metalinguistic tasks from Beguš et al. (2023). We further fine-tuned the 8B model using 4-bit QLoRA (Dettmers et al., 2024) with the following hyperparameters: a learning rate of 7e-4, a batch size of 16, three epochs, and the AdamW optimizer. Due to computational constraints, we evaluated the 70B model using a few-shot in-context learning with 4, 8, and 16 examples. These examples were randomly sampled from the test set and presented to the model in random order to prevent potential sequence-related biases. We assess both models' performance when asked to assume two distinct roles: a language teacher and a forensic linguist. LLM experiments employed three-fold cross-validation due to computational constraints. Based on previous studies on the TOEFL dataset, lower-fold cross-validation typically yields more variable accuracy scores, though differences are generally small (1-3%) (Malmasi and Dras, 2018). Details of the fine-tuning setup and the system prompt are provided in Appendix A.1.

5 Results and Discussion

We present our key experimental findings through two main analyses. First, Table 2 shows the performance of LLMs on TOEFL4 in different configurations. Second, we assess cross-domain generalization by evaluating these TOEFL4-trained models on ICLE4-NLI, with results presented in Table 3.

System + Features	Acc (%)
POS 1-3 grams $_{ML}$	76.2
LLaMA-3.1-8B$_{full}$	64.3
LLaMA-3.1-70B$_{full}$	96.5
LLaMA-3.1-8B$_{POS-ZS}$	26.0
LLaMA-3.1-70B$_{POS-ZS}$	55.2
LLaMA-3.1-70B$_{POS-FS@4}$	58.4
LLaMA-3.1-70B$_{POS-FS@8}$	63.2
LLaMA-3.1-70B$_{POS-FS@16}$	63.5
LLaMA-3.1-8B$_{POS-FT}$	**89.2**

Table 2: The accuracy score for systems, comparing syntactic features (POS n-grams, DT-grams), combined features (POS + DT-grams) and LLM analysis of (LLaMA 3.1 8B and 70B). ZS: Zero-shot, FS: Few-shot, FT: Fine-tuned, ML: Machine Learning (SVM)

5.1 Performance of LLMs

We demonstrate that the impressive zero-shot performance of LLMs (96.5%) on the TOEFL4 benchmark (LLaMA-3.1-70B$_{full}$) drops to 55.2% when the content words are masked with their POS tags (LLaMA-3.1-70B$_{POS-ZS}$) excluding function words and punctuation marks. While few-shot prompting with L1-specific examples improves performance, we observe diminishing returns beyond 16 examples. This setup also significantly increases the computational overhead, as transformer models' memory and computation requirements scale quadratically with input sequence. Furthermore, zero-shot performance ($POS - ZS$) falls short of the traditional machine learning baseline trained on POS n-grams (ML), suggesting that the model struggles to fully capture the linguistic patterns present in the text. However, after fine-tuning, the 8B parameter model achieves an accuracy of 89.2%, a performance that proves robust even in cross-domain evaluation. This represents a considerable advance over previous approaches, which typically showed substantial performance degradation when tested with out-of-domain data, as shown in Table 3 (TOEFL4→ICLE). Our analysis revealed that the prompt for the role of language teacher achieved higher performance in zero-shot settings (53.1%) compared to the role of forensic linguist (55.2%), with this difference being statistically significant ($p < 0.03$).

System	ICLE	TOEFL4→ICLE
POS 1-3 grams $_{ML}$	-	62.1
LLaMA-3.1-8B$_{ZS}$	30.1	-
LLaMA-3.1-70B$_{ZS}$	64.3	-
LLaMA-3.1-8B$_{FT}$	95.6	**90.3**

Table 3: The accuracy scores (%) on ICLE4 dataset, comparing in-domain performance with cross-domain transfer from TOEFL4. ZS: Zero-shot, FT: Fine-tuned, ML: Machine Learning (SVM)

For zero shot settings, the primary challenge was differentiating between the pair of French and Italian languages, as detailed in the confusion matrix presented in Figure 1. The model exhibits a systematic bias toward Italian predictions under uncertainty, resulting in a notably low prediction accuracy for both French and Spanish L1 texts. Although few-shot prompting partially mitigates this limitation by improving French L1 identification, the confusion between Romance languages persists. This pattern can be attributed to two key factors: first, language learners from these

Romance language backgrounds exhibit similar error patterns in their English writing; second, our content-masking approach prevents the model from leveraging distinctive lexical cues such as false friends. In contrast, German L1 texts were consistently the most accurately identified in all approaches. This superior performance can be potentially explained by several linguistic factors: The transfer effects of German L1 learners are more structurally distinct. Importantly, our prompt design, which explicitly mentions "German" as a classification label, may guide the model to search for these distinctive features even under content-masked conditions. For instance, German L1 writers show characteristic patterns in their use of function words (e.g., unique placement of "that" in subordinate clauses) and delexicalized verbs (e.g., distinct usage patterns of "make" and "do" influenced by German "machen"). These systematic differences, particularly visible in the syntactic structures preserved by our replacement approach, possibly make German L1 texts more readily distinguishable from Romance language backgrounds. To verify this hypothesis about the role of function words in L1 identification, future work could extend the masking approach to replace function words with their corresponding POS tags.

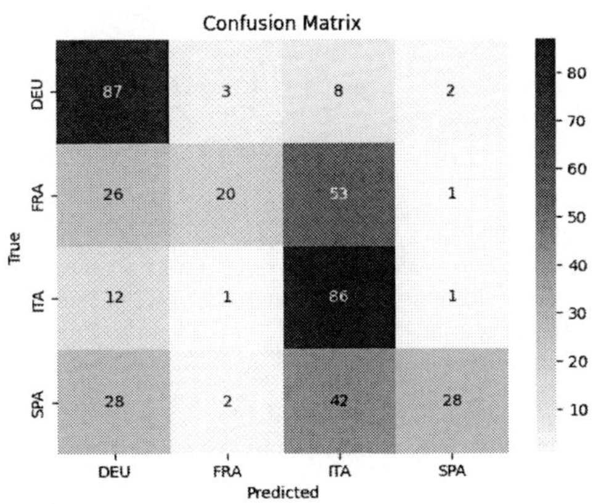

Figure 1: Confusion matrix of the model LLaMA3.1-70B under zero-shot settings. The results highlight the distribution of predictions across different L1.

5.2 Model Interpretation

One of the main criticisms of LLM is their lack of explainability, as their output often does not transparently reflect their underlying reasoning processes (Turpin et al., 2024). For exploratory analysis, we provide an example NLI analysis completed by LLM in Appendix A.3. The linguistic features most frequently mentioned in these analyses are summarized in Table 4. Assessing the significance of these features involves studying the self-consistency of the model by removing or perturbing specific features and evaluating their impact on classification (Parcalabescu and Frank, 2024), which we leave for future work.

Category	Occurrences (%)
Word Order and Sentence Structure	491 (30.66)
Prepositions	359 (22.42)
Grammatical Errors	260 (16.24)
Syntactic Patterns	195 (12.18)
Idiomatic Expressions and Phrasing	177 (11.06)
Articles and Determiners	132 (8.24)
Error Patterns and Miscellaneous	107 (6.68)
Pronouns	104 (6.50)
Function Words	80 (5.00)
Vocabulary and Lexical Choices	29 (1.81)

Table 4: Frequency Distribution of Linguistic Features in Generated Analysis (Llama-3.1-70B)

Traditional SLA research has relied heavily on inherently interpretable models, such as the linear SVM baseline used in our study. These models allow researchers to directly examine the coefficients to identify the most significant features for classification, providing clear insights into cross-linguistic influences from different backgrounds of L1 (Berti et al., 2023). In particular, many features identified in LLM outputs align closely with the findings of these traditional models and are well documented in the SLA literature. This suggests that model behavior may resemble a form of approximate retrieval, where the models reference documents containing these linguistic structures to derive their classifications.

Our analysis of the best-performing zero-shot model's results for German L1 writers (the most accurately identified background) illustrates this alignment through three distinctive features. German writers employ the expletive construction ("there is") more frequently than writers from other L1 backgrounds in the TOEFL-4 dataset. They demonstrate a clear preference for complex sentences, characterized by frequent use of relative clauses ("N which") and generally more intricate syntactic structures. They show a distinctive pattern in their use of impersonal expressions, particularly through the use of "one," often appearing in fixed expressions like "man kann sagen" (translated as "one can say," commonly used to mean "in conclusion" or "I think"). These patterns not only align with the findings of traditional SLA research, but also emerge consistently in LLM outputs, suggesting an ability to identify and leverage meaningful linguistic features.

6 Conclusion

Our study makes significant contributions to understanding LLMs' linguistic abilities in native language identification. Although LLMs have shown impressive performance in NLI tasks on various benchmarks, our investigation reveals a more nuanced picture when evaluating their ability to analyze structural linguistic features in isolation. The dramatic performance drop when content words are masked (from 96.5% to 55.2% for LLaMA-3.1-70B) suggests that these models heavily rely on lexical and content-based cues in their initial predictions. However, through further fine-tuning in these controlled settings, models can achieve an accuracy of 89.2% with strong generalization across domains. These findings reveal that LLMs can acquire structural analysis capabilities through fine-tuning. Our results contribute to the growing body of evidence that LLMs can exhibit metalinguistic abilities, as demonstrated not only through their performance on formal linguistic tasks but also through their capabilities in downstream applications such as NLI.

Limitations

Experimental Design: Our evaluation is focused solely on NLI as a proxy of metalinguistic competence, which may not capture the full spectrum of linguistic abilities and understanding. The controlled setup using POS tags and function words cannot fully represent the complex interactions between syntax, morphology, semantics, and pragmatics in natural language.

Dataset Coverage: The study's reliance on TOEFL11 and ICLE4-NLI datasets with only four L1 backgrounds (French, German, Italian, Spanish) limits the generalizability of our findings across different languages.

Practical Applications: While our findings demonstrate promising results in controlled settings, their applicability to real-world forensic linguistics or educational applications requires further investigation.

Ethics Statement

Our project only processes information from publicly available learner corpora. No sensitive personal data was accessed, stored, or processed at any stage of the project. The study was granted an ethics board review exemption under the University of Zurich guidelines.

Acknowledgments

This work was supported by the collaboration between the University of Zurich and PRODAFT as part of the Innosuisse innovation project AUCH 103.188 IP-ICT (Author profiling to automatize attribution in cybercrime investigations). The authors thank Prof. Rico Sennrich from the University of Zurich for his exchange of ideas.

References

Chirag Agarwal, Sree Harsha Tanneru, and Himabindu Lakkaraju. 2024. Faithfulness vs. plausibility: On the (un) reliability of explanations from large language models. *arXiv preprint arXiv:2402.04614*.

Gašper Beguš, Maksymilian Dąbkowski, and Ryan Rhodes. 2023. Large linguistic models: Analyzing theoretical linguistic abilities of llms. *arXiv preprint arXiv:2305.00948*.

Yonatan Belinkov. 2022. Probing classifiers: Promises, shortcomings, and advances. *Computational Linguistics*, 48(1):207–219.

Beatrice Benelli, Carmen Belacchi, Gianluca Gini, and Daniela Lucangeli. 2006. 'to define means to say what you know about things': the development of definitional skills as metalinguistic acquisition. *Journal of Child Language*, 33(1):71–97.

Barbara Berti, Andrea Esuli, and Fabrizio Sebastiani. 2023. Unravelling interlanguage facts via explainable machine learning. *Digital Scholarship in the Humanities*, 38(3):953–977.

D Blanchard. 2013. TOEFL11: A Corpus of Non-native English. *Educational Testing Service*.

Tim Dettmers, Artidoro Pagnoni, Ari Holtzman, and Luke Zettlemoyer. 2024. Qlora: Efficient finetuning of quantized llms. *Advances in Neural Information Processing Systems*, 36.

Sylviane Granger, Estelle Dagneaux, Fanny Meunier, and Magali Paquot. 2009. *International Corpus of Learner English. Version 2. Handbook.*

Oren Halvani and Lukas Graner. 2021. Posnoise: An effective countermeasure against topic biases in authorship analysis. In *Proceedings of the 16th International Conference on Availability, Reliability and Security*, pages 1–12.

Shunichi Ishihara, Sonia Kulkarni, Michael Carne, Sabine Ehrhardt, and Andrea Nini. 2024. Validation in forensic text comparison: Issues and opportunities. *Languages*, 9(2):47.

Khaled Karim and Hossein Nassaji. 2020. The revision and transfer effects of direct and indirect comprehensive corrective feedback on esl students' writing. *Language Teaching Research*, 24(4):519–539.

Shervin Malmasi and Mark Dras. 2018. Native language identification with classifier stacking and ensembles. *Computational Linguistics*, 44(3):403–446.

Shervin Malmasi, Keelan Evanini, Aoife Cahill, Joel Tetreault, Robert Pugh, Christopher Hamill, Diane Napolitano, and Yao Qian. 2017. A report on the 2017 native language identification shared task. In *Proceedings of the 12th Workshop on Innovative Use of NLP for Building Educational Applications*, pages 62–75.

Ilia Markov, Vivi Nastase, and Carlo Strapparava. 2022. Exploiting native language interference for native language identification. *Natural Language Engineering*, 28(2):167–197.

Raphaël Millière. 2024. Language models as models of language. *arXiv preprint arXiv:2408.07144*.

Maria Nadejde and Joel Tetreault. 2020. Personalizing grammatical error correction: Adaptation to proficiency level and l1. *arXiv preprint arXiv:2006.02964*.

Yee Man Ng and Ilia Markov. 2024. Leveraging open-source large language models for native language identification. *arXiv preprint arXiv:2409.09659*.

Andrea Nini, Oren Halvani, Lukas Graner, Valerio Gherardi, and Shunichi Ishihara. 2024. Authorship verification based on the likelihood ratio of grammar models. *arXiv preprint arXiv:2403.08462*.

Joel Nothman, Hanmin Qin, and Roman Yurchak. 2018. Stop word lists in free open-source software packages. In *Proceedings of workshop for NLP open source software (NLP-OSS)*, pages 7–12.

Letitia Parcalabescu and Anette Frank. 2024. On measuring faithfulness or self-consistency of natural language explanations. In *Proceedings of the 62nd Annual Meeting of the Association for Computational Linguistics (Volume 1: Long Papers)*, pages 6048–6089.

Fabian Pedregosa, Gaël Varoquaux, Alexandre Gramfort, Vincent Michel, Bertrand Thirion, Olivier Grisel, Mathieu Blondel, Peter Prettenhofer, Ron Weiss, Vincent Dubourg, et al. 2011. Scikit-learn: Machine learning in python. *the Journal of machine Learning research*, 12:2825–2830.

Miles Turpin, Julian Michael, Ethan Perez, and Samuel Bowman. 2024. Language models don't always say what they think: unfaithful explanations in chain-of-thought prompting. *Advances in Neural Information Processing Systems*, 36.

Ahmet Yavuz Uluslu and Gerold Schneider. 2022. Scaling native language identification with transformer adapters. *arXiv preprint arXiv:2211.10117*.

Ahmet Yavuz Uluslu, Gerold Schneider, and Can Yildizli. 2024. Native language identification improves authorship attribution. In *Proceedings of the 7th International Conference on Natural Language and Speech Processing (ICNLSP 2024)*, pages 297–303.

Matias Johansen Vian. 2023. A study of transformers for cross-corpus native language identification. Master's thesis, NTNU.

Andreas Waldis, Yotam Perlitz, Leshem Choshen, Yufang Hou, and Iryna Gurevych. 2024. Holmes: Benchmark the linguistic competence of language models. *arXiv preprint arXiv:2404.18923*.

Liming Yu and Terence Odlin. 2016. *New perspectives on transfer in second language learning*, volume 92. Multilingual Matters.

Wei Zhang and Alexandre Salle. 2023. Native language identification with large language models. *arXiv preprint arXiv:2312.07819*.

A Appendix – Supplementary Material

A.1 LLM Prompts and Outputs

You are a forensic linguist/**language teacher** that reads English texts written by non-native speakers in order to identify their native language. Use clues such as word choice patterns, syntactic structures, and grammatical errors to determine the author's native language. You will analyze texts where all content words have been replaced with specific POS tags:
- NOUN -> N
- PROPN (Proper Noun) -> P
- VERB -> V
- ADJ (Adjective) -> J
- ADV (Adverb) -> B
- NUM (Number) -> D
- SYM (Symbol) -> S

All function words remain unchanged. Analyze this new text and identify the native language of the author from among four possibilities: Italian (ITA), Spanish (SPA), French (FRA), or German (DEU).

Figure A.1: System Prompts 1-2

```
### Instruction:
<system prompt>
### Input:
<TOEFL11 ESSAY TEXT>
### Response:
<L1 LABEL>
```

Figure A.2: Fine-tuning Prompt

Analyzing the provided text, I've identified several clues that suggest the author's native language is German (DEU). Here are the key indicators:

1. **Word order:** German often uses a subject-object-verb word order, especially in subordinate clauses. In the text, we see phrases like "i think it is an J N and in the following N you will V my N about this" and "when i think about all this it would be the J to make now V what we should do with the N". This word order is more typical of German than the other options.

2. **Use of modal verbs:** German often uses modal verbs like "können" (can) and "müssen" (must) in a way that's different from the other languages. In the text, we see phrases like "N can also go by N" and "it would be a J N for the N and N J when less N V the N with N and N". This use of modal verbs is more typical of German.

3. **Clause structure:** German often uses complex clause structures with multiple subordinate clauses. In the text, we see phrases like "my J N is that it would be a J N for the N and N J when less N V the N with N and N" and "when i think about all this it would be the J to make now V what we should do with the N". This complex clause structure is more typical of German.

4. **Lack of articles:** German often omits articles in certain contexts, especially in informal writing. In the text, we see phrases like "i think it is an J N" and "N can also go by N". This lack of articles is more typical of German.

5. **Use of prepositions:** German often uses prepositions like "mit" (with) and "von" (from) in a way that's different from the other languages. In the text, we see phrases like "N can also go by N, N and N or by N or V B with other N in one N" and "B it could be a N in D N for us to V N with N from N or N". This use of prepositions is more typical of German.

Based on these clues, I conclude that the author's native language is German (DEU).

Figure A.3: An example linguistic analysis generated by LLaMA-3.1-70B.

Association for Computational Linguistics
209 N. Eighth Street
Stroudsburg, Pennsylvania 18360

ISBN 979-8-3313-1887-1

CURRAN ASSOCIATES INC.
proceedings.com